Beyond Hunger
A Biblical Mandate for Social Responsibility

ART BEALS
WITH LARRY LIBBY

MULTNOMAH · PRESS
Portland, Oregon 97266

Unless otherwise indicated, all Scripture quotations are from the Holy Bible: New International Version, © 1978 by the International Bible Society.

Cover design and illustration by Britt Taylor Collins

BEYOND HUNGER
© 1985 by Arthur Beals
Published by Multnomah Press
Portland, Oregon 97266

Printed in the United States of America

Library of Congress Cataloging in Publication Data

Beals, Art.
  Beyond hunger.

  Includes index.
  1. Church and the poor—Developing countries.   2. Distributive justice—Religious aspects—Christianity.   3. Beals, Art.
4. Developing countries—Church history.   I. Libby, Larry.   II. Title.
BV639.P6B4   1985   261.8'325   85-4912
ISBN 0-88070-098-X

85 86 87 88 89 90 91 – 10 9 8 7 6 5 4 3 2 1

To Mark Andrew,
my first-born son,
whose inquiring mind,
restless spirit,
and penetrating questions
caused me to rethink the gospel
and thereby discover God's
special concern for the poor
and oppressed.

Contents

Foreword

World hunger is on the rise. Poverty and starvation are critical problems facing much of the world. The spectre of famine has cast its shadow over us all. But the average American's existence is too far removed from the poor and starving of Africa and Asia to allow them to fully comprehend the extent of these problems. In this book, Art Beals attempts to present the realities of poverty and starvation, painting vivid pictures of the suffering and despair that characterize the lives of so many of the world's peoples.

Forty thousand children worldwide die of starvation every day—seven thousand to ten thousand per day in Africa alone at the time of this writing. As Christians, how often do we pause to really consider these statistics? What meaning, one may wonder, do they have in relation to our everyday lives?

The United States is the wealthiest nation in the world. While we must be thankful for our abundance, it is important that we remember our Christian responsibility to help the hungry and poverty-stricken. As Proverbs 21:13 states, "If a man shuts his ears to the cry of the poor, he too will cry out and not be answered." How often we hear such cries and do not heed them!

The images of starving children appear in the news virtually every day. The plight of the homeless and poverty-stricken in our own country is witness to the universality of these problems. How much have we done to relieve their suffering? Have we heeded their call? Is compassion fatigue taking over?

In 1974, I had the privilege of spending a day in the presence of Mother Teresa of the Missionaries of Charity. In the context of a suffering world, she is one who clearly witnesses the influence of the living God in daily life. She is an inspiring example of the way the love of Jesus Christ can touch so many through a dedicated servant.

As my family and I toured Calcutta with Mother Teresa, we visited the orphanage filled with crippled children, the so-called "House of Dying," where the sick and diseased are cared for in their last days, and the dispensary, where the poor line up by the hundreds to receive badly needed basic medical attention. Mother Teresa ministered to these people, feeding and nursing the sick and elderly, loving them when others had left them to die. I was overwhelmed by the sheer magnitude of the suffering and the utter impossibility of the tasks which Mother Teresa and her coworkers face daily. "How can you bear the load without being crushed by the impossibility of the task?" I asked. "My dear Senator," replied Mother Teresa, "I am not called to be successful; I am called to be faithful."

How often we lose sight of that fact! So often we are discouraged by the problems of the world and convinced there is nothing we can do to help solve them, so we avoid any action at all. Indeed, Jesus said that the poor always would be with us. We will never be able to completely eradicate hunger and poverty in our lifetime.

Our responsibility, however, is to do what we can to help others gain true freedom through Jesus Christ. One key to this freedom is human development. Christian organizations, such as World Concern and World Vision, work to bring relief to the poor and starving people of the world and to share with them the skills of human development that will allow them to achieve self-reliance in meeting their basic individual and community needs.

The message of this book is clear: As believers in the power of Christ, we must work to minimize the injustice in the world. We must strive to feed the hungry and clothe and house the poor. We must share the necessary skills that will enable them to reach their full human potential.

This book is an inspiration. It encourages all Christians to heed the call of those in need. We should keep in mind Jesus' exhortation to "Love your neighbor as yourself" when he tells the story of the good Samaritan. When many others had passed the robbed and beaten man on the roadside, the good Samaritan stopped and ministered to him. The Samaritan was a true neighbor, heeding the call of another in need, regardless of the risk or cost to himself.

As Christians, we must live in the light of the saving grace of Christ our Lord, ministering to those in need and loving our neighbor as ourselves. As Art Beals writes, "In the faces of the poor and hungry, we will find the face of Christ. For as he said, 'I assure you that whatever you did for the humblest of my brothers, you did for me.'"

Mark O. Hatfield
United States Senate

Preface

"God and Groceries!"

That was a title I selected for a Sunday morning sermon over ten years ago. While there is nothing profound about the phrase itself, that sermon did mark a profound change that was taking place in my thinking—a shift in my understanding of the gospel itself.

For months I had been wrestling with a question: If the gospel is "good news," isn't it because it has something to say to *all* of life—and not just spiritual concerns? And so it was that on this particular Sunday morning in the early 1970s, I felt ready to share my broadened understanding with my congregation at Portland's First Baptist Church. The sermon, which will never be remembered as a classic, was an important milestone for me: it reflected the integration I had discovered in the physical and the spiritual, the social and the religious, in evangelism and social concern.

This harmony in the fundamental gospel message was *not* a part of my religious background or training. Social concern (I had thought) was something best left to those who were either confused in their theology or simply didn't care about theology!

Six years of pastoral ministry in the United States and ten years of evangelism and church-planting in the Philippines had been my training ground up until this point in my ministry. Pressing family needs necessitated a return home. The new ministry of this thriving downtown church became, for me, a new laboratory of learning. The hurts we had experienced within our own family bred a new sensitivity to the hurts of others. And daily I discovered that during my ten year absence deep changes had taken place in this country I called home. The civil rights movement, campus rebellion, anti-war demonstrations, poverty in the inner city, and the new drug culture drove me to read more broadly, study more intently, and question more courageously than I ever had before. Where was the relevance for the changeless gospel in such a rapidly changing society? I began looking at my world—and my Bible—with new eyes. Did God have anything to say about the despoiling of the world's environment, world hunger, the population crisis, or the unjust distribution of the earth's resources?

This struggle became the crucible for a new season of learning in my life—as well as the focus for a concerned ministry which attempted, however feebly, to bring the "good news" to meet the physical, social, and economic needs of people while ministering to their spiritual needs.

In mid 1975 I left the traditional pastoral ministry to develop a new Christian ministry, World Concern. My 9 years of leadership in this evangelical relief and development agency has been the catalyst for ideas expressed in this book. Rather than being a compendium of my thoughts and ideas, this book is more of a journal—tracing my journey to bring an authentic healing ministry to a hurting and broken world.

In these years, traveling in eighty-five countries of the third and fourth worlds and ministering alongside our relief and refugee workers in famine, war, and disaster situations, I have found my easy answers dying. More and more I have asked God to grant me a deeper understanding of the gospel in all its implications.

Planning strategies with third world Christian believers, enabling them to gain better control over their life situations, has broadened my understanding of world need, of God's grace and mercy, and of the enormous creativity within the body of Christ to enable and empower people to live as God intended. Together we have listened to the voice of the Holy Spirit.

Working with the "new missionary," the relief and development professional, I have seen doors once closed to the gospel swing wide open. Traditional forms of Christian witness are not always permissible in rigid Muslim, Hindu, or Buddhist cultures. But as God's love becomes incarnated once again in the flesh and blood of his compassionate children, giving the "cup of cold water in my name" becomes a powerful instrument for Christian witness. Experiencing the joy of a group of impoverished believers as they discover solutions for their severe social or economic problems brings enormous satisfaction and great thanksgiving to the Lord who is rich and plenteous in mercy.

My greatest desire in life is to better understand and communicate this gospel of wholeness. Just as Jesus "went everywhere preaching the good news of the kingdom of God, healing every kind of disease and sickness," we must strive to present him in his wholeness to a broken and dying world. I hope this book will help you on your journey. Writing it has helped me on mine!

Acknowledgments

So many have contributed so much to make this book a reality. If my former colleagues, Richard Perry and Tim Burgess, had not encouraged me to write this book, I would never have had the confidence or courage. Every member of the World Concern team has made some special contribution: a cogent thought, a shared experience, a listening ear, an enthusiastic spirit. A special thanks belongs to my personal secretary, Bernice Dreher, who helped organize me as I tried to organize my thoughts and material. I also express my great appreciation with the several women in word processing both at World Concern and Multnomah Press who have had the *imagination* to decipher the scrawls submitted as manuscript.

Larry Libby, a gifted writer and personal friend, has lived with me through the experience of writing this book. We traveled together in Calcutta and Dhaka and Kathmandu. If he was willing to use his giftedness as a writer to facilitate me in writing, I wanted him to experience my world. We were both changed by the experience! Larry has listened patiently as I've tried out my ideas on him, has prodded me when I grew weary in the task, and has encouraged me when I knew that "writing is not for me—I'm a verbal communicator!" Thanks, dear brother, for not giving up on me. Larry's contribution in editing, rewriting, and in bringing color when the text got a little heavy brought fresh life to my words and experience.

But all of these contributions would have been insufficient had I not had a wife and children who have sacrificed much in order to release me for this ministry of healing. Sonia, my dear and faithful wife, has stood beside me through the years. She has brought encouragement in my moments of despair and balance in my times of excess. She has lovingly borne with my weaknesses and helped me develop my strengths. She has provided wisdom and realism to an incurable optimist who sees only opportunities without problems, challenges without obstacles. Sonia, your steady faith and constant love always help me through my worst times of self-doubt and discouragement. I would have quit halfway through chapter 1 without you!

And my kids. Mark, Karen, Paul, and Beth. You're all grown now, with your own lives. But we've shared life together. We've encouraged each other to ask the tough questions. We have willingly exposed our pain and have worked hard to be honest with each other. You have helped me to see people as they are, to love the unlovable, to seek forthright answers for troubling questions, and to try to live a life worthy of his high calling, to be fully open to God's unspeakable gift of love!

PART 1

*"For I was hungry and you gave me something to eat,
I was thirsty and you gave me something to drink,
I was a stranger and you invited me in,
I needed clothes and you clothed me,
I was sick and you looked after me,
I was in prison and you came to visit me"*
(Matthew 25:35, 36).

"The poor you will always have with you" (Matthew 26:11).

Chapter 1

The Face of the Poor

*I*t all looked a little unreal. Like an oversized Cecil B. DeMille movie lot.

But this was no staged extravaganza, no cinematic illusion. I was watching it happen—right before my unbelieving eyes.

And the tens of thousands of people who came streaming out of the Cambodian jungle weren't paid Hollywood extras. They were bewildered men, women, and children. Very real. Very frightened. And very hungry.

They kept coming and coming. Multitudes. Masses. Endless lines of what appeared to be carelessly clothed skeletons, drawn across the miles by the promise of food at Nong Chan, a refugee settlement on the border of Thailand and Cambodia. Some had journeyed for days, others for weeks. It was difficult to believe that our medical teams could keep them alive long enough for them to profit from the offered food.

But on they came. Pushing their carts, driving their oxen, bearing buckets strung on bamboo poles carried across bony shoulders. Thirty-five to fifty thousand of them poured into Nong Chan every day, accepted their meager ration of food, and then returned.

21

How can you identify with that kind of poverty and those kinds of numbers? You can't. Neither could I. But then I looked into the face of one person . . . and everything changed.

THE FACE OF A BROKEN MOTHER

She was a poor, hungry mother. And she stopped long enough to tell her story through an interpreter. She and her family had lived in Phnom Penh, Cambodia's capital city. The entire populace had been driven from the city by the dreaded Khmer Rouge. While the woman looked on with horror, the soldiers dragged her shopkeeper husband into the street and shot him. His only crime? He wore eyeglasses. This "proved" that he was a "dangerous intellectual," ready to subvert the revolution. But the horror didn't end there. Tearing her six-month-old daughter and eighteen-month-old son from her grasp, the soldiers tossed the infants into the air and caught them on the end of their bayonets.

Numb with terror and sorrow, she was herded into the countryside where she saw open graves filled with hundreds of corpses, lying where they have been mowed down by machine gun fire. A planned genocide of a gentle people.

Suddenly, from the mind-boggling crowds of barefoot peasants, I saw one person. And looking into the face of one single poor person will change anyone's perspective. The rationales and reasons so often given to explain away poverty and hunger no longer had any meaning. There was something about this mother's misery that made me feel responsible. Responsible for living such an uncaring life; responsible to do everything I could to alleviate such suffering; responsible just to care.

A face . . . just one troubled face among so many.

A TERRIBLE CHOICE

Another face floats into my memory, the face of a simple Vietnamese fisherman.

I had been standing on Hong Kong's government dock with two World Relief workers as a frail, battered fishing boat pulled alongside. Men, women, and children began climbing over the side of the vessel and pulling themselves onto the dock. Boat people.

Five, six, seven, eight . . . they came ashore in a gray, driving rain, taking cautious, tentative steps on the first firm ground under their feet for almost six weeks.

Twenty-six, twenty-seven, twenty-eight . . . where could they all be coming from? The boat couldn't have been longer than twenty-four feet—no more than eight feet across at the beam. It should have carried ten people at the most.

Fifty-one, fifty-two, fifty-three, fifty-four . . . my mind rebelled at what my eyes were telling me. Finally the decks were emptied of their human mass, but—rough boards on the deck were pulled aside and the whole interior of the hull was filled with people! Thirty-two more of them crawled out and staggered onto the dock.

I retched as the stench from the craft suddenly enveloped me: the putrid smells of eighty-six human beings living for thirty-eight days with no sanitary facilities.

Hong Kong's governor stood beside me, shaking his head. "You would have to want freedom very much to risk your life aboard one of these boats," he said.

And immediately after those eighty-six refugees had scrambled ashore, another boat took the first boat's place. Eleven such battered vessels were waiting their turn to dock and unload their human cargo.

"One night we had sixty-eight boats with more than 2,900 refugees aboard arrive in Hong Kong's waters," a government official told me. "Right now they are coming in at a thousand a day."

Just as the thought of those numbers started to overwhelm me, I met the fisherman.

He was only one individual—one young father—in that sea of distressed humanity. But looking into his face . . . my perspective changed.

He introduced me to his fourteen-year-old son and his two daughters, aged seven and five.

"We had made arrangements months ago for this fishing boat," he explained to me through an interpreter. "Twenty-four of us sold everything we had to purchase the boat.

"The night we had planned to leave was perfect. No moon, and heavy clouds were draped across the sky. I swam out through the surf with my young daughters holding on around my neck. My son swam alongside. My wife was just a few strokes behind. I lifted the two girls out of the water to be received by helping hands on board. I turned back to give my wife a hand but—she was struggling back to shore—screaming hysterically—terrified by the darkness and the sea.

"I called to her but either she didn't hear me or her terror didn't let her respond. Just as I started back to get her, the boat began to shove off! I tried to stop it! I tried to persuade my wife. Then I had to make an awful choice. My son could care for himself—but not my two little girls. So I made my choice. I'll probably never see my wife again."

"BRING YOUR EYES AND SEE"

The poor. The oppressed. Perhaps you've read the statistics, seen the graphs, and considered the staggering numbers. *But have you ever looked into their faces?* An old Somali proverb says, "You will not believe until you see. You must bring your eyes and look on the problem and then you will go away and believe."

I've seen the poor.

I've seen them crowded and hungry in wretched *favelas*, paper-walled shacks clinging to dusty hillsides in the suburbs of Rio de Janeiro. Whenever I sit for a moment in the darkened squalor of their shanties, I am reminded of the huts I used to build as a child. What adventure to carefully nail together boards and sticks pirated away from my father's garage. Carefully I would tack up cement bags, packing materials, bits of plywood and sheet-metal left over from some of Dad's home improvement schemes. Soon, in my childhood imagination, the fabricated hut became my new fantasy home. Here I was in charge. I could leave reality for awhile and become doctor, lawyer, merchant, chief. Just a little imagination!

But there is no fantasy for the poor. There is no retreat from the dilapidated shack in a steamy urban slum in Calcutta, Cairo, Madras, Manila, São Paulo, or San Salvador. And those who live inside—they all bear the same face of desperation and despair.

I remember seeing a family of eight living on the streets of Calcutta. Flies and filth covered their bodies and their few possessions. "Home" was forty-eight square feet marked out on the sidewalk. "Privacy" was turning one's back on the crowd passing by on a busy urban sidewalk. Water was carried from a broken tap two blocks down the street. Meals, if there was food today, were cooked over a small fire fueled by leftover coal from a rich man's fire. Food had been scavenged from the mounds of decaying garbage piled on every street corner. Toilet and teeth brushing, laundry and bathing, sleeping and loving and playing—all done in forty-eight square feet on the public pavement!

O CALCUTTA!

As many as one million of the homeless poor live out their lives in hopeless desperation on these sidewalks and streets of Calcutta. Early each morning large trucks rumble along the avenues and alleyways to collect the bodies of those who never awakened to another day of monotonous, dehumanizing poverty.

And in the face of each member of this family of eight, I see the same lines of hopelessness and despair. I see the gaunt frame, the hollow cheeks and sunken eyes which form the mask of malnutrition. And in those eyes . . . you look into them and think, "Something's wrong. Something's missing."

Something *is* missing. You look in vain for any glimmer of hope—any spark of life, humor, expectation, tenderness. All of these have been quenched by the daily pressure of simply staying alive in an environment so pungent with the sounds and smells of urban poverty.

Calcutta, a microcosm, represents the poor and dying of our world. Every evil known by humankind, every form of greed, perversity, and injustice is manifest here daily. The sobs of its battered and abused women, the moans of its dying, the whimper of its homeless children, the curses of its men dehumanized by a lifetime of unemployment, these are the sounds of two hundred million of the world's people who live each day of their lives in absolute poverty.

On a recent visit to Calcutta, while visiting a children's home supported by World Concern, I was taken by the director to visit the slums where several of these children came from. Until then, I could not understand how mothers could desert their young.

After a few minutes visiting these slums . . . I understood.

Home for these children was a mud hovel. The doorway could only be entered by stooping low to the ground. One could not stand erect in the shelter. Inside it was dark, airless. Hot and humid. Fetid with the smells of human waste and rotting garbage.

I wondered how anyone could survive in such an impoverished environment. But this was home for an entire family of eight! The worker introduced me to the mother. I saw a woman who was wasted by years of toil and childbearing—malnourished for want of food while still nursing her latest offspring. She had been repeatedly abused over the years by a drunken husband, a man whose only means of coping with *his* despair was to dull the pain and his mind by drinking a potent, home-brewed drink. She had been driven to a point beyond desperation—a place where a mother will even desert her young in order to survive and to provide an opportunity for the abandoned children.

Call her a statistic. Call her children statistics. A point on some obscure government chart, a mark on some United Nations bar graph. But the fact is, she is real. The children are real. And so is their pain.

A WORLD OF NEED

Most of us don't respond to statistics. Numbers can be so bloodless—so detached from any sense of reality. And yet the statistics are there, figures which speak of an aching world. Each day 42,000 of the world's children die needlessly because of hunger and easily preventable childhood diseases.

One billion of the world's people live in conditions of absolute poverty without even the most basic resources available. No adequate food, clothing, shelter, education, or medical care.

Four hundred million persons are severely malnourished, more than 200 million of these the world's children. Fifty million boys and girls have suffered permanent brain damage just because they did not have adequate protein in their diet during the first five years of their lives.

Two billion, or almost half the world's population, earn less than $300 per person each year. In many of the less developed countries, twenty-five percent of the working population are unemployed and another twenty-five percent are *under* employed—holding jobs whose pay scales are not adequate to finance even the most basic needs of life.

Today there are more than 600 million poor in Asia, Africa, and Latin America who are landless. Each year that number grows. Before the turn of the century, that number will have increased to over one billion. Millions of these will be refugees with neither land nor citizenship! Other scores of millions will be city dwellers, living in squalid urban slums. By the end of this century, it is estimated that thirty-nine percent of all Africans, seventy-five percent of all Latin Americans, and forty-seven percent of all Asians will be living in cities, cities where large population groups live in the most wretched conditions available.

How easy it is, as one scans through these statistics, to form unfair opinions. How easy it is to make judgments about the poor when one has never seen their faces, never looked into their eyes. How simple to explain away poverty when one has never felt its pain.

THE MYTHS OF POVERTY

I've heard every explanation of poverty imaginable.

"If only they would have fewer children!"

And how many children would a North American family give birth to if they knew that half of these children would die before reaching age five, and half of the remaining children would die from hunger and preventable disease before they reached their teen years?

How many children would the parents of families in the developed countries bear if they knew that their male offspring were their only future—the hands to help push the plow, their only guarantee of continuity, their only life insurance, medical insurance, and retirement? Would their attitude change?

"These people need to change their religion. These false religions are what create poverty."

I might respond to a comment like that by directing the individual's attention to a country like the Philippines—a country with a population eighty-five percent Catholic, the only major third world country which as a colony was molded by American education, business, and government know-how. Today, more than fifty percent of Filipino children are malnourished, and it's strange . . . but I've never found that non-Christian poverty looks any different from the poverty experienced by the children of these poor rural peasants seeking out an existence in some remote barrio.

Two of the world's *richest* economies are in countries where Muslim religion predominates. One cannot assign poverty or affluence to religious belief. Geography, history, and culture, as well as political and economic power, are far more determinative economic factors.

In a nationally syndicated newspaper column entitled "Let the Poor Feed Themselves," the American journalist Paul Harvey commented on the relationship between people's religious beliefs and poverty.

"There is no way that you and I are ever going to comprehend a society that feeds cows and starves babies," Harvey writes, speaking of the land of India and his understanding of the Hindu religion's sacred cows.

But one could wonder which culture, India's or affluent Western nations', has the most "sacred cows." While our "sacred cows" are not part of our recognizable religious traditions, American families feed their cattle 1800 pounds of protein-rich grain in order to produce 250 pounds of meat for our dinner table.

In light of this, one might ask which culture is more guilty of feeding cows and starving babies. For the protein-rich grains of our verdant farmlands can often mean the difference between life and death for millions in the famine-afflicted regions of our world.

"The problem is their economic system. Capitalism and free enterprise will eliminate poverty."

Really? Ask the sons and daughters of tenant farmers in Central America who struggle to survive while cultivating lush farmlands which produce food for overfed citizens in the developed world. Ask the jobless in America's urban slums, the unemployed in a small eastern seaboard or midwestern town economically dependent on a dying industry whose factories are obsolete, whose market has been captured by foreign competition. Ask the leaders of any third world nation whose fundamental economic reality is paying their interest payments on burgeoning national debts while they try to keep transportation and small industry fueled with imported petroleum products whose price has escalated ten-fold in ten years!

"The poor are just lazy. If only they had a better work ethic there wouldn't be so much poverty."

It's really difficult to work long hours in tropical heat and humidity when there is no food to eat before leaving for work in the fields . . . when young bodies are weakened by parasites and disease resulting from polluted drinking water, crowded, unhealthy slum conditions, diets that never contain sufficient calories, protein, vitamins, and minerals to build strong bodies. A living condition of absolute poverty and an environment of hopelessness is not a productive seedbed to nurture a strong sense of self-reliance and personal initiative.

EASY ANSWERS

It's really quite safe to parrot easy answers about the root causes of poverty, hunger, and disease while living in isolation from the hurts and suffering of more than half of the world's people.

Too many people "know all the answers" before they've even understood the real questions.

But if we "listen up" in our world . . . if we strain to hear the human family's feeble, desperate cry for some kind of humane response from another brother, then we will see the face of the poor in a new light, a personal light. It is impossible for us to develop a compassionate understanding of the plight of the poor until we step out of anonymity and apathy in order to become *involved* with them, in order to see the faces of poverty, in order to feel their hurt, in order to take the suffering of another and make it our own.

ONE MORE GUILT TRIP?

Many times since assuming responsibility for leadership in a Christian relief and development agency, I have had people come up to me and say, "Please don't send me any more of your letters or magazines. I just can't stand those pictures of malnourished children . . . those faces of thousands of refugees huddled in crowded camps."

We often feel a need to protect ourselves from the facts, the realities, fearing that these will hurl us downward into "one more guilt trip."

While I always assure these people that it is not our policy to force our communications on any person, to remove their name from a mailing list will solve nothing. The poor will not go away simply because we refuse to acknowledge their existence. Closing one's eyes will not alter the reality of suffering for millions of men, women, and children living in conditions not fit for any human.

We *do* need to know the hurts of those who live on the desperate edge of starvation.

We *do* need to feel their pain.

We need not more guilt, but an enlightened concern which will move us to action. All too often guilt is nothing more than an unhealthy emotional response to a conviction *not* acted upon.

THE POOR ARE REAL PEOPLE

It really makes little difference what "face" the poor man wears.

The peasant farmer struggling with homemade crutches, walking down dusty roads to the refugee hospital to receive medical care, the stump of his amputated foot and lower leg covered with someone's discarded plastic lunch bag.

The leprosy victim, sitting in "untouchable" loneliness in the putrid, dark underpass of a Madras, India, street.

The Somali grandmother gathering thornbush and grass to fabricate a simple hut which will provide shelter for her pregnant daughter and orphaned grandchildren.

A landless Manobo tribesman in the Southern Philippines struggling to cut back the jungle in order to cultivate a little corn and rice for his family. He knows only too well that in another month or year, powerful, "civilized" farmers from the lowlands will crowd him further into the jungle while government officials look on with little interest other than their own greedy self-interest.

The unemployed father living in a crowded urban slum, despair written across his face. He had come to the city with his family to survive, only to find that crowded cities provide less opportunity than over-crowded, too-small parcels of farmland in the countryside.

A Haitian farmer trying to eke out an existence, tilling the rocky soil on a steep hillside, knowing that no matter how hard he works, there will never be enough to feed his entire family. Some will have to go to bed hungry tonight. They do every night.

These are the faces of the poor.

They are easy to find in any number of poor countries in our world.

I've tried to rationalize them away, but I cannot forget them. I dare not!

I have felt pity for them, only to realize that pity helps me keep my emotional distance from them.

I have extended sympathy, only to discover that sympathy is my passport maintained to protect my cultural advantages. It serves to separate me from the poor rather than identify me with their sufferings.

Then there are those positive moments of time when I feel compassion, that personal, intimate involvement with the poor and those who suffer. In those moments I begin to understand the words of Jesus. "The poor," he said, "you will always have with you."

What did he mean? He was not speaking some cold, hard reality. He was not shrugging his shoulders, saying, "Well, that's the way it's always been, that's the way it'll always be. Que sera, sera."

No. He was speaking in regard to our responsibility. The poor *are* always with us. And we need to know them, to understand their feelings, to feel their pain, to struggle to save them from the malevolent forces of poverty which control their lives and their future.

How easy it is to form opinions of the poor when we have never looked into their faces!

The psalmist calls us to "Defend the cause of the weak and fatherless; maintain the rights of the poor and oppressed. Rescue the weak and needy" (Psalm 82:3-4).

Jesus came to preach "good news to the poor" (Luke 4:18).

The wise writer of the Proverbs warns, "If a man shuts his ears to the cry of the poor, he too will cry out and not be answered" (Proverbs 21:13).

To oppress the poor is to insult our Maker (cf. Proverbs 14:31), and the one who closes his ears to their cries will find that Jehovah will not hear his own cry in a time of need!

*"When Jesus saw the crowds,
he had compassion on them . . ."*
(Matthew 9:36).

Chapter 2

The Face of Compassion

*I*t was a mid-winter night and cold for Bangladesh. Each night temperatures dipped to about forty-two degrees in the capital city of Dhaka. This was my first visit to this part of the world. Ten years of living in the Philippines had done little to prepare me for the overwhelming reality of human suffering I was experiencing in this impoverished land.

Years of war followed by cyclones and floods had left this crowded, suffering country with few of the resources needed to cope with the simplest challenges of daily existence.

During Bangladesh's fight for independence, millions had been slaughtered. One-third of the nation's more than seventy million were left homeless. Hundreds of thousands of its women had been brutally raped, many left with children fathered by men in the departing armies. Most of the country's intellectuals had been executed.

Then followed two of this century's most devastating cyclones and tidal waves. In two successive years these tragic national disasters had wiped out more than eighty percent of Bangladesh's rice harvest. Hundreds of thousands of people were devoured by a terrifying wall of water pushed by winds from the Bay of Bengal. Scores of villages along with their people and animals ceased to exist in just a few minutes of time.

CRUSHED AND IN DESPAIR

The storms receded, but the horror and misery did not.

Death continued to stalk Bangladesh, this time wearing the garb of hunger. Because of the dislocation of war and flood, and the famine resulting from destroyed crops, millions starved. Surviving millions roamed the countryside in search of food and shelter. Hundreds of thousands crowded into the old city of Dhaka, hoping that the city could provide solutions.

But they did not find help. They found only multitudes of others just like themselves—desperate human beings ravaged by hopelessness, hunger, homelessness, and sorrow.

You could sense the broken spirit of the people on that cold night in Dhaka. I accompanied Bangladeshi and expatriate relief workers while they made their rounds of mercy. Periodically during the evening, the drivers would stop our Land Rover under a group of trees on some darkened street. In just moments, large groups of half-naked, hungry refugees would crowd around us, pushing and shoving in order to get to the front of the row in hopes of receiving some bread or rice and milk. Most of the women were carrying naked young children and babies. No covering at all from the penetrating chill of the night.

I was spared the impact of their suffering by the sheer pressure of work. So many to be fed . . . so many children to be clothed. I remember thinking that my experience that night gave real meaning to my "calling" as a Christian relief and development executive! This was what this caring ministry was created to do: "To feed the hungry, clothe the naked."

Hours later our food and clothing supplies were depleted, and our relief team was exhausted.

I returned to the shelter of my hotel room. But sleep never came. I tossed uncomfortably in my bed. I reasoned with God about the injustice of these dear people's suffering—sobbing with anger and frustration—overwhelmed by the magnitude of the need and the scarcity of resources to help.

These experiences continued for four days and nights. And for four nights I lay in my bed weeping . . . weeping for the suffering ones. Weeping for me. Despair washed over me in sickening waves every night, and did not ebb away at dawn.

HOPE WHERE THERE IS NO HOPE

On my final day in Bangladesh, I visited Tongi—a huge refugee camp outside the city. More than 40,000 of the most impoverished refugees were sheltered in this camp. Several Christian relief and development agencies were supplying food and medical services, administering feeding programs, attempting to stave off the seemingly inevitable.

Death comes slowly and silently to the starving.

That morning I helped serve the famished mothers and children as they stood patiently in endless lines, waiting to receive their cup of milk and two protein-enriched biscuits. A few old men were allowed to join the line. The teen-aged boys and the men were expected to go to the city and fend for themselves.

Finally it was more than I could bear. I turned my back on the relief activity, the hungry children, the endless lines, the desperate mothers clutching starving babies in their fragile arms. I cried, quietly, but with little concern for control.

"Dear God," I said between sobs, "it's all so hopeless! We feed one line and two more form. Feed them today and what will they do tomorrow? There isn't sufficient food to give them. We have to choose which days we can feed. The zoos in America are far more effective—and regular in feeding—than we can be here. There is no hope in all this despair. Dear God, don't you really care?"

A seasoned relief worker from India overheard my tearful prayer. He placed a gentle arm on my shoulder and smiled at me.

"Hopeless?" he said. "Oh no, Art. It's not hopeless. Don't

you see it? There is hope everywhere!"

My unexpressed response was one of, "You've got to be kidding, man. Look around you."

"See that old man over there?" My friend pointed, and I looked. I saw a gnarled old man, his skeletal frame bent over from the years of heavy burdens carried on his back. His hands cradled two protein biscuits and a small glass of milk. His face shone with a toothless smile which seemed to radiate all the pleasure and delight of a young child at a birthday party!

"You see, Art, there is hope everywhere in this wretched camp. You just have to look for it. That old man was awakened this morning by the gnawing pangs of hunger. He had no food yesterday and no promise of food today. But now the food has come. If there is food today, there may be food tomorrow. He awoke with nothing, now he lives with something. This is hope!"

I guess one calls this hope reduced to its lowest common denominator.

PITY ... OR COMPASSION?

I learned a profound lesson that day about hope—a lesson which has helped me keep my perspective on human suffering and tragedy through the years. The lesson is this: Hope springs from a heart of compassion; despair is the product of a heart full of pity.

While visiting the United Nations office for refugee work in Somalia, I was struck by the words of a poster on one of the walls:
THE REFUGEE PROBLEM ISN'T HOPELESS.
UNLESS YOU THINK SO!

The rational side of me wanted to summarily reject those words. Suffering Somalia was a land of a million refugees. Already the fourth poorest country in the world, its population had suddenly soared by almost twenty-five percent. And its new "residents" were homeless, utterly impoverished refugees.

People with nothing. With those facts in view, it was far easier to experience feelings of hopelessness rather than hope and optimism.

Nevertheless, the words of the poster stayed with me. I have begun to appreciate the subtle wisdom of the message. It actually came close to paralleling an important bit of wisdom I learned during my first visit to the People's Republic of China. One of my government hosts, speaking of a crisis involving many thousands of homeless peasants, told me that I could learn an important lesson from China.

I was eager to learn such a lesson, so I listened carefully as he explained. The Chinese language, he told me, is written in word pictures. Each word is expressed by one or more characters. The word *crisis* in Chinese is made up of two characters. The first character is the one used to express *danger*. The second character means *opportunity*.

How profound! Every crisis is made up of two components—danger and opportunity. The seeds of hope, then, are sown in every crisis. You just have to look for them!

COPING . . . OR CARING?

While I was visiting a Christian development worker in Nepal, he told me of a conversation a Nepalese friend of his had had with His Majesty, the King of Nepal. Despite Nepal's massive social, economic, and ecological problems, the king is doing all he can to better the life of the people of his kingdom. But progress comes painfully slow. The king commented to my friend about the way the poor Nepalese peasant learned to cope with suffering and deprivation.

"My people," said the king, "tend to live more with hope than with reality."

This is probably all too true. But those who are the observers of another's suffering are often just as much removed from reality. People can usually be divided into three groups: those who just don't know what is happening, those who observe what is happening (but whose lives are left uninfluenced), and those choice few who really make things happen.

Hope is that great ingredient which will turn the confused or the uncaring into people of action—compassionate action!

EMOTIONS . . . OR ACTION?

I've learned the profound difference between pity and compassion.

> Pity weeps and walks away,
> compassion comes to help and stay!

That's it! Pity, you see, is an emotional response. Compassion is an action response.

Pity touches our *feelings*. Compassion engages our *will*.

Pity often produces the tears that help us keep a safe distance from another's problem. Compassion provides that bridge which helps us move from our background and experiences—from "our position"—to embrace the hurts and cares of another.

Pity observes. Compassion involves.

One quickly learns the difference by observing people's response to suffering and poverty. I remember all too well the evangelical tourists I guided through Manila during my years of missionary service. We usually began our tour with the more typical tourist spots of that enchanting Asian city. Then we would visit "the work"—Christian radio stations, churches, Bible colleges and seminaries, home Bible study groups.

But always, I took them to the slums.

This was the "other side" of the city few tourists ever see. Hundreds of thousands of Manila's citizenry live in appalling conditions. Paper shacks, open sewers, filth and garbage everywhere. Crowded living conditions a westerner finds difficult to comprehend.

The tourists listened, looked, and snapped their pictures.

Their response was predictable as they thanked me at the conclusion of the slum section of the tour.

"I will *never* forget what you have shown me today. I never knew people lived in such conditions."

But all too often they did forget. Never forgetting to give thanks to the tour guide, they were able to forget the people, the wretched living conditions, the anguish of poverty. The experience became nothing more than one of many snapshots to show the folks back home.

It's always that way. Pity weeps . . . but walks away. Compassion weeps, too. But then it stays around to help.

Pity understands that there are two hundred million severely malnourished children in our world. Compassion recognizes the opportunity one has to live with a little less so others might live. It finds ways to provide food rather than merely learn about world hunger. It understands that just as children die— one at a time—they can be helped in the same way.

Pity rails against the injustice of discrimination. Compassion alters life styles in order to focus personal resources which can be used in caring for disadvantaged people.

Pity observes human suffering. Compassion suffers with those who suffer.

COMPASSION OBSERVED

Jesus and his disciples traveled through all the towns and villages of Galilee. He taught in their synagogues. He preached the good news of the Kingdom of God. And when he saw the crowds, "he had compassion on them, because they were harassed and helpless, like sheep without a shepherd" (Matthew 9:36).

The Son of God did not merely "weep and walk away" when he observed earth's suffering from the heavens. He *came*. He came to help. To stay. To pitch his tent among us. To pour out his very life for those who hurt and suffer.

He saw people under the political bondage of Rome, and he was concerned.

He saw people under the religious bondage of the

Pharisees, and he was concerned.

He saw people under the grinding bondage of the Evil One—living out their days under the shadow of sin and death—and he was concerned.

He came not to be ministered unto, but to minister. It was his compassion, his merciful heart that caused him to relate to the burdens and sorrows of his people.

Once a man with leprosy came and knelt before Jesus.

"Lord, if you are willing, you can make me clean" (Matthew 8:2).

And Jesus was willing. He reached out his hand, touched the man, spoke the word, and the man was healed.

Touched. That's a word of personal involvement. No theological or religious requirements before the healing. No impersonal, rational explanations of the disease and the prescriptions for healing. He simply reached out and touched.

If we would walk in his steps, we must do the same.

HIGH TECH . . . HIGH TOUCH

In John Nesbitt's best seller, *Megatrends*, he observes that western civilization is in the midst of a technological revolution. Just as surely as civilization moved from a primitive society to an agricultural society and the agricultural society gave way to the industrial society, today life rushes toward a high-technology society. This technology often desensitizes and depersonalizes life. In order to sensitize and personalize human relationships today, Nesbitt predicts, a "high-touch" society will emerge.

But there is really nothing new under the sun. Today the computer is blamed for the high-tech society. But there was, in one sense, a highly technical society in Jesus' day. Not one resulting from electronic computers, but from religious legalism. The "good news" had become lost in a technical thicket of laws, prohibitions, and empty traditions.

Jesus came to restore the "touch" to life. Caring, feeling, reaching, and touching, Jesus ministered to the physical, emotional, and spiritual needs of those he came to serve.

A ruler of the synagogue came and knelt before Jesus. Looking up at the Teacher from Galilee, he blurted out his request. The man's little daughter was ill—at the point of death. And he believed that Jesus was the one who could make the difference.

Our Lord's response?

No questions asked. No standards for belief elaborated. No paperwork in triplicate. No queries to determine the worthiness of the individual or the worthwhileness of the task.

"Jesus got up and went with him. . . . he went in and took the girl by the hand" (Matthew 9:19, 25). And the girl was healed.

Compassion is an action response. It demands direct involvement.

The disciples really wanted to serve. After all, had they not left all to follow Jesus? But all too often their response to need, human need, never rose above a response of pity. They saw the Samaritan woman at the well. But they said nothing, their silence wishing her removed. Jesus, however, ministered to her deepest needs—socially and spiritually (John 4).

When Jesus spent a full day teaching the multitudes, the disciples discerned the gnawing physical hunger of the people. Their "solution" was to send them away! Jesus, however, wishing to show forth the glory of God, multiplied the resources that were at hand and sent the people home full! (John 6).

A woman came, having suffered many things from many physicians for many years. The disciples wished to protect Jesus from the crowd, like Secret Service men forming a cordon around an American president. Jesus, however, was sensitive to the touch of one woman. In compassion he reached out and healed her (Luke 8).

Crowds brought their babies to Jesus to have him touch them. They understood the power of a compassionate touch!

The disciples rebuked them and wished to send them away. Jesus, however, called the children to him and reminded the disciples that unless they became as these children, they would not enter the kingdom of God (Luke 18).

Amazingly, while the crowds clamored for his attention, Jesus always focused his attention upon the individual—doing the work of the kingdom one-to-one. What value he placed on one solitary life! He still does.

In Somalia, I have seen Christian doctors and nurses with this same focus. They help thousands of refugee children and adults—they pray with mothers who are grieving over the death of a child, they comfort those separated from their homeland, dying from disease. And always one-at-a-time.

On a small, rocky island off the coast of Malaysia, I observed one of our "touch agents" at work. She sits with the children—they are called unaccompanied minors, the forgotten ones. Cuddling them in her arms, she smiles, talks, laughs, and cares. And the parentless children respond. They no longer feel alone. Fear loses its paralyzing terror. They begin to feel loved again. The therapy of a loving touch.

> You hear, O Lord, the desire of the afflicted;
>> you encourage them, and you listen to their cry,
> defending the fatherless and the oppressed,
>> in order that man, who is of the earth, may terrify
>> no more.
>
> (Psalm 10:17-18)

What a contrast between those who observe human need, who learn all the statistics of hunger, who crusade for the "poor and oppressed," and those who, in compassion, simply reach out and touch.

KNOWING AND CARING

People who are suffering don't really care how much we know until they know how much we really care. We can learn all about the problem and gather information about solutions, but only when our concerns are translated into compassionate actions will we be able to heal some of the hurts of our world. Dr. Bob Pierce, the founder of World Vision, prayed for that compassionate heart. He had seen the death and destruction of life in Korea. He asked for a heart "that would be broken by the things that break the heart of God." And that compassion translated into action today ministers to millions of suffering people all over the world.

True compassion is an action response.

DANGER: COMPASSION WILL BREAK YOUR HEART!

Pity sees the world as it is, broken, hopeless, and dying. Compassion has the potential not only to feel the hurts, but to experience the hope. When our emotional response to suffering is one of pity, we wish to remain separated from the problem, isolated and sheltered.

A few years ago I took an evangelical American book editor on his first trip to India. Touring some impoverished areas in the southern tip of the sub-continent, we stopped the car at an encampment of desperately poor gypsies. My friend had come all the way to India to see the work of relief and development among the poor . . . but didn't want to get out of the car!

I could understand. We all have a built-in defense mechanism which protects us from the unpleasantness we either do not wish to deal with—or don't know how to deal with.

Compassion, however, takes the offensive. In broken-heartedness, we commit ourselves to become involved, to feel the pain, and to work for healing. Once, when talking with Bishop Festo Kivengere, the Anglican bishop of Uganda who has seen and experienced so much hurt and pain in that broken land, he said of those who expressed pity over the suffering of Ugandan Christians, "Some of us become overwhelmed before we've begun."

Pity is the response that comes when you've never begun.

Compassion sees a beginning point for ministry rather than an ending point to trouble. Human need is not an impenetrable wall of despair; it is the door which swings wide open to bring God's best, man's best, the world's best into action.

It's easy to see the wall—that dark, formidable barrier of seemingly hopeless poverty and human suffering. But our Christian faith sees *a door in the wall*. That's the good news. The door, however, is in the shape of a cross. From a human perspective, that's bad news.

Let me explain: The cross-as-a-door picture is a biblical image seen in the experience of God's Son. "Let us fix our eyes on Jesus . . . who for the *joy* set before him endured the cross. . . . Consider him who endured such opposition . . . so that you will not grow weary and lose heart" (Hebrews 12:2, 3).

He saw the joy—the hope, the solution—before him, *but he always viewed it through the cross*. That which could have been the greatest obstacle, the most humiliating defeat, the deepest horror, became the most beautiful door of all eternity.

And if our heart is a heart of compassion, we can experience the same. We can see with the eyes of Jesus. All too often the doors of opportunity and hope swing on hinges of suffering, pain, sorrow. From this perspective, however, the cross becomes a doorway rather than a barrier; an opening, not a closure.

As Jesus viewed the cross, he could always see beyond it to that "joy set before him." And by looking—really looking—into the face of the poor, we can experience the same, "the joy set before us." Compassion sees the world as Jesus sees it: not only broken, but redeemable! Rather than inciting pity, suffering can give birth to hope—a hope that becomes the foundation for all compassionate action.

Looking at the worst from a compassionate viewpoint will help us discover the best in human behavior. The world could produce no Mother Teresas if it had no Calcuttas of human misery. This viewpoint can move us from pity to compassion, from despair to hope, from paralysis to participation. With compassionate hearts and a perspective of hope, we can move forward into a hurting world and cause real change. I know; I've seen it happen.

IN HIS NAME

The world is far too fearsome a place, and there is far too much at stake for us to insulate ourselves in comfort and turn away from the needs of crushed and impoverished people. To become involved will often break your heart, but it will also provide a whole new center of being, a new purpose for living.

Those who have seen me work long hours in distressing situations to help the hurts of the poor have asked me, "Art, how do you take it? How can you bear up under the crushing burden of human misery?"

The answer is simply "a compassionate heart." And here we will avoid compassion "burn-out." We burn out not from overexposure to the problems, but from underexposure to the solutions.

It's easy to be problem-oriented. To be compassionate is to be solution-oriented. The compassionate heart acknowledges that one can't do everything . . . but one can do *something*. And knowing that, it takes risks to find solutions, to help bear the load . . . to love . . . to touch . . . and to feel, in Jesus' name.

*"They were harassed and helpless,
like sheep without a shepherd"* (Matthew 9:36).

Chapter 3

The Face of Oppression

*H*arassed and helpless!
Foreign armies of occupation controlled their land. The imperial head was far away in a distant country, but its power and presence were pervasive in every part of life. Heavy taxation kept the people forever in debt to a government that cared little for their needs.

Ownership of land was the right of a small minority who had made their peace with this foreign presence. In the best years one could scarcely earn enough from the land to care for just the most basic family needs.

Any small infraction of the law—even when the law was not known or not understood—was dealt with mechanically, severely, and without mercy.

On one side, the citizens of that occupied land were victimized by fellow countrymen only too willing to sell out to the colonial masters—traitors who would stop at nothing for personal gain. On the other side were the "liberators," those who claimed to represent "the people" in their back-alley campaign of terror and violence. But all too often it was the innocent who suffered. Those who did their best to live quiet lives, who

49

wanted only to live and work and watch their children grow . . . these were the ones who would be caught in the crossfire of a war they wanted nothing to do with.

Then there were the religious leaders.

They spoke such eloquent words, prayed such learned prayers, cast such an impressive image in their robes and vestments. But somehow the God they represented seemed far away, unconcerned, even passive. And the rules and regulations and observances were hard to bear—one more heavy load for shoulders already weighed down and weary.

Life itself could be so overwhelming—so many aches and sorrows and pressures. It was hard to relate to a religion dominated by traditions of the past, a religion that studiously ignored a common man's everyday struggles and longings and needs. These theologians—these distinguished, distant doctors of the law—seemed obsessed with dotting i's and crossing t's. They had neither the time nor the inclination to feel the hurts, heal the bruises, or cleanse the moral and physical wounds which crushed the spirit and robbed tomorrow of its hope.

These were the people of Capernaum.

Small wonder Jesus called them "harassed and helpless, like sheep without a shepherd." And these Capernaumites are emblematic of so many suffering people in our world today.

VICTIMS OF THE VICTORS

Think of the twelve to sixteen million refugees around our globe this very hour. Victims of war, famine, political and economic oppression, they roam the face of the earth trying to find security in an environment where there are no homes, no jobs, no government to defend a citizen's rights, no regular food, shelter, education, or medical care.

Worst of all, there is no real hope for the future.

Harassed and helpless! Sheep without a shepherd.

Our generation has seen more than its share of refugees. Within the past decade severe refugee problems have afflicted large population groups on every continent.

BEYOND DESPAIR

I have stood alongside Christian refugee workers in the border camps of Thailand. Here, hundreds of thousands of Laotian and Cambodian refugees have fled war, famine, and political oppression. Diseased in body, broken in spirit, without any resources for living, they have risked life and limb in order to pursue their hopes for freedom and opportunity.

I can never forget the young mother—a boat person from Vietnam—I interviewed in a refugee camp in Malaysia. Her husband, if he was still alive, was in a communist prison. His only crime was his years of service in a war Americans had grown weary of. Twice her boat had been stopped on the high seas by Thai pirates. They had raped all the women on board. The men were shot and dumped into the sea with two of this mother's children—thrown overboard alive, never seen again. Her body heaved as she sobbed out her story to the camp social worker.

You simply can't empathize with that kind of powerless, hopeless despair until you've seen it firsthand.

Harassed and helpless! She was like a sheep without a shepherd.

A ROLL CALL OF REFUGEES

Who are these homeless ones . . . these rootless, jobless, often helpless wanderers? Where do they come from? Where are they going? Today's roll call of refugees will be different from tomorrow's. By the time this book goes to print others will be added to the list. The geographical locations will vary, but other features will be all too familiar . . . ravaged hopes, blasted lives, and hungry, desperate faces.

One might head today's list with millions of Cambodians, Laotians, and Vietnamese, refugees created by decades of violence and oppression in Indochina.

It would include several million Afghan refugees living in crowded camps along the border of Pakistan, victims of communist expansion and local government complicity.

We could add more than one million refugees from Ethiopia who have fled to Somalia, victims of warfare in the Ogaden desert, a region claimed by both governments. This is a war—like so many others—increased in its horror through the intervention of major military powers on both sides of the disputed political issue.

Hundreds of thousands of Ugandan Christians fled the genocidal terror of Idi Amin; many still wander. Tribalism and religious fanaticism increase their terror.

Cuban boat people and Haitians continue to flee the grinding oppression of dictatorial regimes. Political refugees from despotic governments in Chile and Argentina add to the ceaseless flow, as do El Salvadorian refugees seeking shelter from both right-wing death squads and left-wing guerrillas. Miskito Indians look for peace in the dubious security of Honduras, while the Nicaraguan Sandinista revolution runs amok, violating the human rights of this impoverished minority.

The homeless ones also include Guatemalan city-dwellers escaping the terror of army abuses, and rural peasants fleeing to Mexico to escape the demands of Guatemala's "liberating" guerrilla forces. South Africans and Namibians, refugees from the white racist policies of an apartheid government. Angolan refugees fleeing violence, a violence indiscriminately perpetrated by right and left.

The turbulent human river flows on and on, its destructive current and wide-reaching flood plain washing over huge portions of the globe.

Hopeless? *Not unless you think so!* We are not to blame if a person becomes a refugee. We *are* to blame if he continues to be one.

We need eyes to see, ears to hear, minds to inquire, and spirits that understand the plight of the world's refugees. The author of the book of Hebrews wrote with such understanding as he chronicled the plight of an early wave of dispersed, persecuted Jews: "They went about in sheepskins and goatskins, destitute, persecuted and mistreated—the world was not worthy of them. They wandered in deserts and mountains, and in caves and holes in the ground" (Hebrews 11:37, 38).

A world too evil to see the worth of powerless, possession-less refugees . . . a world that somehow could not chart the value of impoverished men, women, and children . . . a world that sounds very much like our own.

THE VIOLENCE OF POVERTY

The evil, the injustice that victimizes so many of the world's people has many causes.

I've seen whole nations torn apart by religious strife, brother killing brother in the name of God. Religious strife between Muslim and Christian . . . Muslim and Hindu . . . Muslim and a variety of religious minorities . . . Muslim and Jew . . . even Muslim against Muslim. Senseless, insane killing, all in the name of certain religious (and political!) beliefs.

But the *violence of poverty* is just as real for those who experience its death-dealing power.

Pause for a moment with an Asian farmer as he rests against his plow in the sapping, humid heat of late afternoon. Experience, just for a moment, this man's frustration—a frustration rooted in his own powerlessness. He has committed no crime, and yet he serves a life sentence of hard labor in the service of a rich, absentee landlord, almost as an indentured slave. He has no alternative. Can we Americans even begin to identify with those words? *No alternative* . . . except starvation for himself and his family.

Listen to his plea. Feel his pain.

He tills the soil all his life—the same soil tilled by his father and his father's father. But the soil does not belong to him! Each year he must borrow money to purchase the seed needed to plant his crops. Each member of the farmer's family engages in the back-breaking toil of plowing and planting, watering and weeding, harvesting and threshing.

If the weather is good, if the plant pests do not destroy, then the harvest is gathered . . . and given to the landowner. One-half to two-thirds of the earnings from the harvest go to the landowner, leaving barely enough to care for the most basic needs of the farmer's family until the next harvest.

Not enough to provide medical care for his wife or young children.

Not enough even to make a small down payment on buying himself out of this perpetual servitude.

And if anything goes wrong . . . drought, flood, illness, plant disease . . . it is the farmer, not the landowner, who will suffer. Now there will not be sufficient funds to feed his entire family. Some will eat and some will not. He must decide. Now there will be no money available to purchase the seed needed to plant the next crop. So the farmer is forced to borrow, usually at exorbitant interest rates, against the next crop. And his indebtedness grows. He literally becomes owned by the land and the landowner. Enslaved for life—and for generations to come.

Harassed and helpless! They are like sheep without a shepherd.

It will take more than a John Deere tractor and North Dakota farming technology, more than "miracle rice," modern fertilizers, and "green revolutions" to deliver these farmers from their economic bondage. There are no simple answers when unjust systems and practices prevail.

A Call for Justice

The prophet Nehemiah spoke out against this type of oppression:

> Now the men and their wives raised a great outcry against their Jewish brothers. Some were saying, "We and our sons and daughters are numerous; in order for us to eat and stay alive, we must get grain."
>
> Others were saying, "We are mortgaging our

fields, our vineyards and our homes to get grain during the famine."

Still others were saying, "We have had to borrow money to pay the king's tax on our fields and vineyards. Although we are of the same flesh and blood as our countrymen and though our sons are as good as theirs, yet we have to subject our sons and daughters to slavery. Some of our daughters have already been enslaved, but we are powerless, because our fields and our vineyards belong to others" (Nehemiah 5:1-5).

When Nehemiah heard the people's complaint, he called for justice. He accused the landowners and the government officials who supported them of usury, extracting unfair and exorbitant interest payments. He accused them of keeping their farming brothers in slavery. And he ordered them to award the land and the profits from the land to those who worked diligently to earn it.

To address such problems as exist today, we need to get a new perspective—a biblical perspective—on ownership. "The earth is the Lord's, and everything in it" (Psalm 24:1). "To the Lord your God belong the heavens, even the highest heavens, the earth and everything in it" (Deuteronomy 10:14). The psalmist enjoins us to "defend the cause of the weak . . . maintain the rights of the poor and oppressed. Rescue the weak and needy" (Psalm 82:3-4). And a wise man once wrote, "A righteous man knows the rights of the poor; a wicked man does not understand such knowledge."

THE RAINBOW PATH . . . TO HELL

The plight of the slum dweller in the large urban center is even more desperate than the plight of the rural farmer.

He has been drawn to the city out of his poverty. Unable to adequately feed his family, doomed to a life of servitude and indebtedness, with no hope to secure the financial means necessary to provide education for his children, the peasant farmer follows the rainbow to the city, only to discover that it's not gold but greater misery at the end of the rainbow.

Yet this false hope moves unprecedented numbers of rural peasants to urban centers. These are the slum dwellers one finds in every world-class city. Their numbers increase alarmingly every day—millions of the world's citizens succumbing to the deceptive allure of the city. Each month they come in ever-increasing numbers. I live in Seattle, a city with a population of about 600,000. The world is producing ten new Seattles each month! And two of these are in Mexico City, now the world's largest city with a population of eighteen million.

In 1980 there were 140 cities with populations in excess of one million. By September 1983 this number had increased to 240 cities. The move to the city is universal in scope. In 1970 the African population was eighty-one percent rural. That number by the end of the century will be reduced to sixty-one percent. Asia will be fifty percent urban by the year 2000.

They move to the city because they have no control over their resources in the rural areas—only to discover they have no real access to resources in the city. Their move to the city is motivated by the weariness which results from year after monotonous year of back-breaking toil. When they arrive, however, they discover only the monotony and desperation of unemployment. An average of twenty-five percent of the population in the cities of developing countries are unemployed, and another twenty-five percent are underemployed.

So the newly arrived rural family moves into the already crowded slum dwelling of relatives or friends. A paper and tin shack. A single water tap on a distant street corner. Open sewers. Fetid heaps of decaying debris. Noise. Pollution. Crime. Prostitution. This is what the hope-filled farmer has received in exchange for his rural poverty. Now he has even less control over his life and future than he had on the farm. He was certain life could not have been any worse—any more unjust—than on the land. But he was wrong. Cruelly, tragically wrong. And there is no going back.

Harassed and helpless! They are like sheep without a shepherd.

A POVERTY OF THE POWERLESS

The God of the Bible is a God of justice! And even as this biblical justice impacts our individual and personal relationships, it must *also* touch those relationships which are economic, political, and social. A private faith which turns its back upon unjust political and social practices is not a biblical faith. The psalmist wrote that God is "a father to the fatherless": he is the God who "remains faithful forever. He upholds the cause of the oppressed and gives food to the hungry. The Lord sets prisoners free" (Psalm 68:5; 146:6, 7).

To speak of personal holiness and to practice injustice is simply hypocrisy. Neither personal faith nor public life can be separated from biblical values.

In speaking of the need for justice in all of life, Julio Santa Ana, a Uruguayan theologian, philosopher, and sociologist, writes:

> The suffering of the poor is not only limited to material needs (scarcity of goods, lack of basic health care services, no real job opportunities, inadequate school facilities and curriculum, absence of basic social systems, etc.). This life is also characterized by dependency and oppression. They have very little opportunity for their own decision-making to shape their lives.
>
> What and when they eat, where and when they work, what wages they should receive and what price they should pay, where and how they should live, how many children they should have and how to bring them up, what they say and how they should

say it, even when they should laugh and when they should cry and how—all these things and many other aspects of life are determined or conditioned by the economic system, political power and religious sanctions controlled by the rich, the powerful and the influential.

Injustice springs from powerlessness, people living without the power to control their lives. Justice is empowering the poor, granting the means whereby they can gain control over their own destinies.

With no power to control their lives, the poor will perpetuate the impoverishment and oppression of those social structures into which they were born. Once a culture of poverty comes into existence, it tends to perpetuate itself from one generation to the next because of its devastating impact upon the children of that culture.

The book *La Vida: A Puerto Rican Family in the Culture of Poverty—San Juan and New York* underlines this point: "By the time slum children are age six or seven they have usually absorbed the basic values and attitudes of their subculture and are not psychologically geared to take full advantage of changing conditions or increased opportunities which may occur in their lifetime." Cultural impoverishment renders them powerless over their environment.

WHAT DOES IT FEEL LIKE TO BE POWERLESS?

How different this is from the sense of power and control the average American feels over his life and surroundings. There have been few times in life when I have found myself in some situation in which I did not have the resources, the intelligence, or the necessary relationships to control the situation. It's simply a fact of American life—and one most of us reared in such a society take for granted.

A few years ago, however, something happened to me in the little Southeast Asian country of Laos that taught me a profound lesson on how it feels to be powerless.

For three days I had been in Laos visiting some of our projects in that impoverished Communist land. Our Thailand director, traveling with me, had cared for the normal travel requirements of government provisions, ministry appointments, and confirmation of travel arrangements outward bound.

Saturday was the day of departure. The plane was scheduled to depart at 2 P.M. Tickets were reconfirmed and the departure time was clearly stated. Because the airport was small (there are few travelers to this small country), and customs-immigration formalities at a minimum, we did not arrive at the airport until forty minutes before the scheduled departure time.

Walking through the entrance, we were surprised to see that the terminal appeared deserted. A virtual ghost town!

Finally a woman government officer came over, and in broken French informed my traveling companion that the flight had left one hour earlier than scheduled.

A look of horror spread across Bill's face. This was Saturday. My flight from Bangkok to Bangladesh was Sunday. He knew that as chairman of a Christian relief and development consortium in Bangladesh, I was scheduled to preside at crucially important meetings on Monday. The government officer informed us that the airport was now closed until the next flight departure on Monday afternoon!

Bill's despair amused me a little. Obviously, he had not encountered these sorts of inconveniences before. Really, it would be no problem. My travels all over the world were filled with little surprises like this. I could always find some alternative, develop some relationship, or take advantage of some different option to keep my forward momentum. It becomes something of a game. "International Travel" . . . roll the dice, take a card, and move forward three spaces. Quite a challenge.

Bill, of course, was embarrassed that he had not checked ahead of time. No problem! We'd just go back to the hotel, dump off our baggage, then go to one of the government ministry offices. We'd arrange something special. Maybe land transportation across the Mekong River into neighboring Thailand—and then an all-night bus ride into Bangkok. Well and good.

Then we ran into the first hitch. The game began to get a shade more complicated.

The travel ministry, it seemed, was closed for the day. And the last ferry across the Mekong was in one hour—but we had to have special government permission to leave the country in that manner.

Go back two spaces and miss a turn.

No problem! A call to the Foreign Minister would fix it. After all, he must have a real appreciation for our organization's medical work at the local leprosy and orthopedic hospitals. I was good at "fixing up" these kinds of problems. All part of the game.

After repeated attempts, several fruitless conversations, and much waste of precious time, we were able to contact the Foreign Minister.

I explained the situation.

The Foreign Minister's reply was polite—but firm. "Our rule states that no foreigner can enter or exit the Democratic People's Republic of Laos except by scheduled airlines. The next flight is Monday afternoon. We will extend your visas to accommodate your extra days of stay. Thank you!"

The game was definitely getting out of hand.

"But you don't understand!" I protested. "I have an important flight connection in Bangkok."

"Sorry."

"Don't you know about the good work we're doing here in Laos?"

"Thank you. Sorry."

"But I'm the chairman of the board of this important relief and development program in Bangladesh. I have to get to the meetings!"

"Impressive! But sorry."

"But all I would have to do is take a taxi eight miles down the road to the ferry crossing and ride across. It would be no problem!"

"Sorry."

By that time I felt tempted to risk the swim! The music from radios in the small Thai village just across the river from my hotel balcony seemed to mock me. So near and yet . . . it might as well have been a hundred miles.

All avenues were now closed to me. My best and final appeal had met with that maddeningly polite indifference. I wasn't going *anywhere* before Monday afternoon and there was absolutely nothing I could do about it! The "game" wasn't fun anymore—because I knew there was no way to win.

For several hours I sat silently on my hotel balcony, listening to the sounds of that Thai village drift across the river, scarcely a stone's throw away but completely out of reach. I did some pondering. What did this situation really mean? I was overwhelmed by feelings of frustration, the emotional fruit of living without the power necessary to control one's destiny.

To this day I am convinced that God allowed this experience in my life for a reason. For the first time in my life I had tasted—just tasted—something of the deep frustration, the sense of utter hopelessness, that comes from the absence of power to control one's life.

Such a small and relatively unimportant incident. And yet what a profound lesson. One billion of the world's people live without the power to make even the simplest choices over the most basic needs of life.

Harassed and helpless! Sheep without a shepherd.

GOD'S PERSPECTIVE

In studying the Scriptures one can find at least 120 biblical texts which teach us that the poor *are* poor because of some kind of oppression. The prophet Isaiah admonishes, "Woe to those who make unjust laws, to those who issue oppressive decrees, to deprive the poor of their rights and rob my oppressed people of justice, making widows their prey and robbing the fatherless" (Isaiah 10:1, 2). The psalmist accused that day's leadership of making injustice legal (Psalm 94:20).

Today, unjust legal systems dispense justice unfairly. The poor have little access to adequate defense under the law. Too often, laws are written to favor the rich and take away from the poor.

Unjust economic structures which unfairly control resources and unequally reward those who are in power perpetuate the poverty of more than half the world's population.

In the early days of the Hebrew nation, God provided a solution for these sorts of encroaching economic injustices—the Year of Jubilee. Every fifty years the people were to return to their own ancestral property. Property lost through indebtedness was returned to its owner.

"The land must not be sold permanently," the Lord told Israel, "because the land is mine and you are but aliens and my tenants" (Leviticus 25:23). If we could only develop God's perspective on ownership, many of the world's injustices would be righted, and we would no longer live in a world where a very small minority of the world's people control the vast majority of the world's resources.

THE LORD STATES HIS CASE

There is something fundamentally unjust about a world economic system in which more than two billion people in the poorest countries live in absolute poverty with incomes of less than $300 annually.

There is little justice in a world in which five percent of the world's population in North America can earn in a lifetime more than forty times as much as more than one billion of America's world neighbors. And we maintain this economic advantage while using twenty times as many of the world's natural resources and contributing fifty times as much to the pollution of the earth's air, land, and water.

In a time of lesser inequities, the prophet Isaiah wrote, "The Lord takes his place in court; he rises to judge the people. The Lord enters into judgment against the elders and leaders of his people: 'It is you who have ruined my vineyard [land and natural resources]; the plunder from the poor is in your houses. What do you mean by crushing my people and grinding the faces of the poor?" (Isaiah 3:13-15).

In the work of development one quickly discovers that there *is* a relationship between how I live and how that affects my brother and sister. The United States has an unusual power to affect the economic future of most of the world's people. The oil crisis of the 1970s demonstrated a direct relationship between three critical factors: one, the price of oil; two, the impact that the level of consumption has on those prices; and three, how those prices affect world economies—especially those of developing countries. Today's third world debt burden and heavy interest payment costs are a direct result of economic changes resulting from the oil crisis.

The average North American is scarcely affected by gasoline prices tripling—or even quadrupling—at the pump. Our price and wage structure make the necessary adjustments. But in subsistence and below subsistence economies where annual income is less than $300, a quadrupling of oil prices has a cascading effect on food prices, on transportation costs, as well as clothing and medical costs . . . but income changes little.

Now a life filled with difficult choices is left with even fewer choices. Forests are denuded, turned into fuel, because the populace can no longer afford kerosene. Subsistence diets are reduced, resulting in severe malnutrition affecting more than 200 million of the world's children. Children die of easily preventable childhood diseases for want of the money needed to purchase basic medications and vaccines. And the spiral of poverty winds ever downward!

Harassed and helpless! They are like sheep without a shepherd.

"MY CHOSEN FAST"

Social injustice, political oppression, unfair taxation policies, racial, sexist, and religous discrimination . . . the litany of injustice is a lengthy one. And these injustices are not limited by geography or characteristics of any one political or economic system. They are universal in their scope, but far more devastating when experienced by the impoverished . . . the powerless.

In a time when religious festivals and observances had been substituted for righteous and just living, the prophet Isaiah reminded the people of God, "Is not this the kind of fasting I have chosen: to loose the chains of injustice and untie the cords of the yoke, to set the oppressed free and break every yoke? Is it not to share your food with the hungry and to provide the poor wanderer with shelter—when you see the naked, to clothe him, and not to turn away from your own flesh and blood?" (Isaiah 58:6-7).

To fully understand and identify with the powerlessness of the poor is to commit oneself to the agenda of Jesus:

To bring the good news of deliverance.

To proclaim freedom to those held captive.

And to let the oppressed go free.

"For I was hungry and you gave me something to eat" (Matthew 25:35).

Chapter 4

The Face of God

Martin Luther had locked himself up in a monk's cell. For two long weeks during Lenten season he denied himself food and drink. In silence, every waking hour, he probed the mystery of one short sentence . . . words wrenched from the tortured soul of a dying man.

At night he slept fitfully as his subconscious mind refused to let go—refused to cease grappling with words and thoughts beyond his reach.

The words had been spoken by Jesus from the cross.

"My God, my God, why have you forsaken me?"

Day after day Luther did nothing but contemplate, pacing back and forth in his cheerless cell. The mystery . . . the fathomless depths . . . the profundity and possibility of those words!

What could they mean?

Did the Son of God really mean this? If not, what *did* he mean? If so, how could the Father do it?

On the fourteenth day he ended his fast and returned to his brothers in the monastery. The first words he spoke were, "God forsaken of God . . . who can understand this?"

There is a sense of this same mystery in Jesus' words to his disciples in Matthew 25. This Olivet discourse is one of the primary teaching passages of Jesus recorded in the gospels. In it he spoke of the end of days, the coming of the Kingdom, and of the need to be ready for these things.

He spoke of end-time judgment as "the dividing of sheep from goats." Those gathered on his left, symbolized as goats, were sent into eternal judgment with these words echoing in their ears: "I was hungry and you gave me nothing to eat, I was thirsty and you gave me nothing to drink, I was a stranger and you did not invite me in, I needed clothes and you did not clothe me, I was sick and in prison and you did not look after me" (Matthew 25:42, 43).

To those on his right, the righteous ones, he assured reward for their faithfulness in doing what those on the left had failed to do. But those at the Lord's right hand were perplexed by the saying. "Lord," they asked, "when did we see you hungry and feed you, or thirsty and give you something to drink?"

The answer was swift in coming. "I tell you the truth, whatever you did for one of the least of these brothers of mine, you did for me."

Can you imagine yourself refusing food to your Lord if he came to your door . . . hungry, in need?

Would you refuse him lodging even if your home was already crowded?

And is there a prison so mean and degrading that you would not happily visit if you knew that your Lord Jesus was incarcerated there?

There is mystery in these words of God's Son—and warning. For the truth, we begin to realize, is that Christ *does* come to us—a thousand times a day. He comes to us as the poor, the hungry and thirsty, the homeless and imprisoned, the despairing and oppressed.

This is a complete reversal from our normal understanding of ministry to the poor. Because Christ gave his life for us, because he gives his love without measure, we gladly serve him by taking his love to those who are impoverished. But here he represents himself *as* the poor!

Our usual formula is: Christ comes to us—we go to the poor. But here it is: Christ comes to us—*we go to him!* He is the poor!

Words of mystery, indeed, but an important truth as we contemplate our responsibility and our opportunity to serve the broken and hurting of our world.

What a difference it would make if we could wrap our minds around this truth. All too often I have gone into the refugee camps, seeing ravaged, grieving masses, and wondered, "Where is God in all this mess?" But understanding this concept, I can return to the camps and find my Lord in the face of that poor refugee, in the eyes of that hungry child. Rather than bitterly questioning his absence, I begin to sense his nearness—the presence of the living Christ.

This understanding brings a new significance in our service to the hopeless, the vulnerable, and the oppressed. Drawing near to them, we draw near to One who loves them.

GOD'S SPECIAL CONCERN FOR THE POOR

Small wonder, then, that so many scriptural passages highlight God's special concern for the poor. Jesus introduces his earthly ministry with the words, "The Spirit of the Lord is on me, because he has anointed me to preach good news to the poor. He has sent me to proclaim freedom for the prisoners and recovery of sight for the blind, to release the oppressed" (Luke 4:18-19).

The Bible speaks of a God who gives security to the oppressed (Psalm 12:5), protecting the weak from the strong and the poor from the oppressor (Psalm 35:10). He is a God who cares for orphans and widows, who gives the lonely a home to live in and leads prisoners into freedom (Psalm 68:5-6). "The Lord hears the needy and does not despise his captive people"

(Psalm 69:33). He "secures justice for the poor and upholds the cause of the needy" (Psalm 140:12).

> The Maker of heaven and earth,
>   the sea, and everything in them—
>   the Lord, who remains faithful forever.
> He upholds the cause of the oppressed
>   and gives food to the hungry.
> The Lord sets prisoners free,
>   the Lord gives sight to the blind,
> the Lord lifts up those who are bowed down,
>   the Lord loves the righteous.
>   (Psalm 146:6-8)

The evidence of God's concern for the poor is everywhere. From the books of history the witness is clear: "He raises the poor from the dust and lifts the needy from the ash heap" (1 Samuel 2:8).

The books of poetry add their testimony: "He saves the needy from the sword . . . he saves them from the clutches of the powerful. So the poor have hope" (Job 5:15, 16). "Who is like the Lord our God . . . He raises the poor from the dust and lifts the needy from the ash heap" (Psalm 113:5, 7).

The prophets, too, give attention to this theme: "The poor and needy search for water . . . I the Lord will answer them" (Isaiah 41:17).

The gospels and epistles of the New Testament add their voice, lest there be any doubt, any questioning. God has a special love and concern for the poor and oppressed. He knows their needs. He feels their pain. And he cares.

THE OTHER FACE OF GOD

In the poor, therefore, we see the face of our God. The Almighty manifests his concern in an identification so complete he is able to tell his followers that to feed the hungry is to actually give bread to God.

But there is another side to the face of God. The apostle Paul refers to this in a reference to Moses' meeting with God on the lonely heights of Sinai. When Moses came face to face with the glory of God, his very flesh took on a celestial radiance.

And in each follower of Jesus Christ there is potential for such radiance, as we "with unveiled faces all reflect the Lord's glory, [we] are being transformed into his likeness with ever-increasing glory" (2 Corinthians 3:18). In a real sense, when we minister to the poor in the power and love of Jesus Christ, we become—to them—the very face of God.

I know this to be true. I have seen the transforming power of a Mother Teresa reflected in the face of a dying beggar, fresh off the streets of Calcutta. This simple peasant woman from Yugoslavia, ministering selflessly to the poor in the name of her risen Lord, has caused the whole world to pause and wonder. And in the lined, craggy features of her face, many have seen the face of Another.

GOD IN FLESH AND BLOOD

God came to this world in flesh and blood in the person of his Son, Jesus Christ. We call this presence *incarnation,* the Almighty God in a human body.

Many stumble over the manner of his birth because it was so poor and humble. He came into this world as little more than a pauper. Few children born in that day had poorer prospects for the future than the one named Jesus of Nazareth. He did not come cloaked in power or wealth or beauty. Instead, he chose to come in weakness, obscurity, and humility. Infinite majesty wrapped in the simple garb of a peasant.

What could we have done . . . had he not come? What would have become of us? We humans, left to ourselves, cannot fix things. We cannot undo the hurt or restrain the monstrous evils we have unleashed across the face of our little world. And no obscure, impersonal deity could have cured us . . . or given us a moment's hope. But God, out of pure love, allowed himself to be born of man, to feel our hurts, drink deeply of our sorrows, and bear the nameless horror of our sin—with all its perversions, rebellions, and twisted selfishness. And by his death he brought healing . . . hope . . . a way out.

And that miracle of *incarnation,* in a spiritual sense, is continued into the present. Indwelt by the Spirit of God, the humblest believer becomes the presence of Christ in a darkened world. We become the face of God to a sin-wracked, dying world.

Mother Teresa of Calcutta understands so well this double miracle of incarnation. In a prayer she composed for Calcutta's Children's Home, she wrote:

> Dearest Lord, may I see you today and every day in the person of your sick, and while nursing them, minister unto you.
>
> Though you hide yourself behind the unattractive disguise of the irritable, the exacting, the unreasonable, may I still recognize you, and say, "Jesus, my patient, how sweet it is to serve you."
>
> Lord, give me this seeing faith, then my work will never become monotonous. I will ever find joy in humoring the fancies and gratifying the wishes of all poor sufferers.
>
> O beloved sick, how doubly dear you are to me, when you personify Christ; and what a privilege is mine to be allowed to tend you.
>
> Sweetest Lord, make me appreciative of the dignity of my high vocation, and its many responsibilities. Never permit me to disgrace it by giving way to coldness, unkindness, or impatience.
>
> And O God, while you are Jesus, my patient, deign also to be to me a patient Jesus, bearing with my faults, looking only to my intention, which is to love and serve you in the person of each of your sick. Amen.

SIMPLE SOLUTIONS TO BIG PROBLEMS

So often we become overwhelmed by the needs of the poor before making any kind of personal commitment to do what we can do to bring about change. It is a delusion to believe that only governments with their power, enormous resources, and state-of-the-art technology can effect change. All too often the very opposite is true. Big problems are often mastered by rather simple solutions.

One of the greatest killers of children in our world is the dehydration resulting from diarrhea. When a child is five or six months old, breast-milk is no longer sufficient to meet the needs of his growing body. If supplementary foods are introduced into the young child's diet at this point, the risk from unsafe water, contaminated foodstuffs, and poor sanitation is very great.

Protecting a child from diarrheal infections is a task no mother in a developing country can accomplish alone. Health and nutrition, education, adequate supplementary foods coupled with methods of hygienic preparation and storage of foods, better personal hygiene on the part of mother and child, all these are needed to guard against these infections. Because these resources are not readily available in many low-income countries, sickness and death result. One out of every twenty children born into the developing world dies of easily preventable diarrhea before reaching age five.

Until recently, the only effective treatment for dehydration was intravenous feeding of solutions administered by qualified medical personnel. Often, however, neither the fluids nor the medical personnel were available, and the child died. But because of the recent discovery of a simple and inexpensive method of preventing or correcting dehydration through ORT (Oral Rehydration Therapy), many of the five million childhood deaths can be prevented. Five hundred million children suffer diarrheal infections three or fewer times each year. Thanks to one of the simplest but most important breakthroughs in medical history, help appears to be at hand. In Guatemala alone, child deaths have been reduced *by half* among a study population involving 64,000 persons. In test villages in Egypt and India, health promoters have experienced the same results. Hospitals in Costa Rica which have employed ORT have reduced deaths by a full eighty percent.

This is just one illustration of a simple solution to a very big problem!

SMALL BEGINNINGS CAN IMPACT NATIONS

From the late 1700s until 1951, the mountain kingdom of Nepal was closed to all foreign influence. This kingdom, extending from the hot plains adjacent to India up to the Himalayan peaks of the world's highest mountains, was in its isolation culturally still living in the Middle Ages.

Then there was a revolution and a new king came to power, a king concerned about the backwardness and extreme poverty of his people. He also cared about his queen. And when she became desperately ill, the king invited a missionary doctor from India to come and minister to her. As a result of this astounding contact with a Christian from the West—the first in almost three hundred years—the door was opened for a small number of professional and technical missionaries to come to Nepal to help the king and his government address some of the most critical physical, social, and economic needs of the people.

While desiring to make Jesus Christ known in word and deed, these early missionary pioneers came with a vision for "nation building." Here was one of the most impoverished countries of the world, a country ravaged by disease, with literally no educational or medical institutions and certainly no programs to take these benefits to the people.

With Hinduism as the national religion and the king venerated as a living Hindu god, it was a culture hostile to Christianity—but open to assistance. These early missionaries saw that in helping the king build his nation, Christ would become known as he revealed himself to the poor and suffering through deeds of mercy. And these missionaries were impelled and compelled by the reality that Christ comes in the person of the hungry and thirsty, the homeless and oppressed.

Have the efforts of this small band of pioneers paid off?

Today these early missionaries have been joined by the sons and daughters of another generation. More than three hundred Christian doctors, nurses, agriculturalists, engineers, teachers, foresters, and veterinarians from more than thirty countries constitute the United Mission to Nepal. Hydroelectric dams, bridges and roads, schools and hospitals, agricultural and community health programs, plywood mills and furniture factories are the tools of their trade used to build the nation, benefit the people, and announce the loving presence of Jesus Christ. In a land that knew no Christians only three decades ago, today there are thousands of believers in hundreds of worshiping communities all across Nepal—a "closed country" with an open heart.

And in this same period of time, through the combined efforts of government and private agencies such as the United Mission to Nepal and the International Nepal Fellowship, real progress has been made, progress which benefits the poor and hungry, the sick and dying. In just two decades, from 1960 to 1980, Nepal's gross domestic product increased six-fold. Infant mortality rates declined a full 25 percent. Even more significantly, the number of deaths among children ages one to four decreased by 35 percent. School enrollment advanced from a small 10 percent of children attending primary school in 1960 to 91 percent of Nepal's children in 1980. The number of young people enrolled in secondary school increased in the same period of time by 350 percent, and the number of literate adults doubled!

All of this after *centuries* of little or no progress in human development. Nepal had entered the twentieth century, and deeply committed Christian professionals with a burning vision to make Christ's love known through word and deed were in the forefront of this significant achievement.

The task of bringing a decent life to Nepal's fifteen million people is far from over. But the work has begun. And because there were Christians who truly believed that Christ comes to us in the poor—that Christ has a special concern for the poor—they have laid the foundation so that a new generation of Christian professionals, working cooperatively with the Nepalese government, can continue to bring that better life to the small mountain villages, the lush agricultural valleys, and the crowded but primitive cities.

LITTLE IS MUCH WHEN GOD IS IN IT!

Massive government programs are not the most effective way to touch and help and heal hurting human beings. Programs come and go. Governments rise and fall. What really makes a difference among the poor is one individual—one life given over to Jesus Christ and his compassion for "sheep without a shepherd."

Dulal Borpujari is such a man.

Born into a Brahmin family in India, Dulal had nothing but a privileged future to look forward to. In a caste system society, he had all the advantages of social position, economic security, and personal power. Through the faithful witness of a Christian wife, however, Dulal's life was transformed by the power of the gospel.

Exchanging a life of ease and security for a life of risk and deprivation, Dulal set out to change his world. Gifted with both mechanical and organizational skills, he invented a plow that would revolutionize farming in India. Simple and inexpensive, this plow had the potential to lift some of the heavy burden of toil from the backs of India's peasant farmers. With a compassion for those "weary and heavy laden," Dulal became successful in the manufacture and marketing of this new kind of plow, which is in wide use all over India to this day. However, through an unfortunate series of events, Dulal was to lose this business and the opportunities that went with it.

God had something bigger for him, something more directly related to "lifting the yoke of oppression, feeding the hungry, and clothing the naked." Dulal had established himself in Calcutta. Sick at heart over the desperate poverty of that city and frustrated with the lack of opportunity for its impoverished young men, Dulal established a vocational training school for boys that not only trains many but also provides employment after training through the manufacture of beds, wheelchairs, and related hospital equipment.

This was only the beginning of a service ministry that would take Dulal Borpujari literally around the world to serve the poor in the name of Jesus Christ. Well-known evangelical relief leader Larry Ward, founder of Food for the Hungry, needed a third-world national with mechanical and technical skills, experienced in business and organization, to manage the affairs of this rapidly growing relief agency in Asia. First in Dhaka, then Bangkok, Dulal managed the famine and refugee projects in many Asian countries. Today, serving as an international vice president, Dulal is just one example of many third-world nationals who have either risen out of poverty or cast aside privilege in order to make an important difference.

RADICALS FOR CHRIST

No bureaucratic government program or well-intentioned foreign aid agency could touch the lives of impoverished Asian men and women in quite the way that Deng and Sucel Samonte do.

Their story begins in the Philippines during the tumultuous years of the late 60s. Government graft and corruption was the rule in those days—not the exception. All too often business placed profits and self-interest above any concern for the people who worked for their companies. Government-sponsored land reforms that had promised much delivered benefits to a very few. Powerful "sugar barons," a land-owner oligarchy which concentrated much of the wealth in fifty prominent families, joined with the profit-making motivations of powerful multi-national cooperatives to create an economic climate of escalating prices, runaway inflation, ridiculously low wages for workers, and small profits for farmers.

Young student radicals took to the streets. There were riots and bombings, demonstrations and car-burnings, strikes and boycotts everywhere. This time of political and social ferment contributed much to the radicalism of two middle-class Filipino students, Deng and Sucel.

Sucel was the daughter of a prominent Manila business couple. Her parents owned and operated a chain of supermarkets in the greater Manila area. Her future was secure. With marketing and advertising degrees she planned to become a key executive in the family business. In her years of study at the University of the Philippines, however, Sucel had developed a strong social conscience, one increasingly influenced by Marxist ideology and anti-American sentiments.

Eduardo Samonte, affectionately called Deng by his many university friends, was a product of the same decade and similar environment. As a student in civil engineering at the same university, he wanted to employ his engineering skills to alleviate the suffering of the oppressed masses. Like Sucel, Deng was of nominal Roman Catholic background, but shared with her a disinterest in religion—an apathy at times tinged with disillusionment and contempt.

From Deng's viewpoint, religion had proved unresponsive to the people's needs and incapable of making any significant, positive change in society.

Deng joined with a group of fellow-activists to do something of real social significance for the slum-dwellers of Tondo, a district of unspeakable poverty and deprivation. He used his skills successfully to build houses for the poor and to design water and sanitation systems to improve the dangerously unsanitary conditions. Tondo was a small district with nearly half a million people crowded into its simple houses and dilapidated shanties.

Becoming friends at the University, Deng and Sucel found a kindred spirit in their concern for the poor. Marriage grew out of the friendship and their commitment to the cause of helping the poor and oppressed. Through a series of near-miraculous events, first Sucel and then Deng came into a personal living relationship with Jesus Christ. Irrelevant, traditional religious ideas were transformed into a personal faith in the saving work of Christ. Fortunately, this conversion experience did not convert them away from their social conscience! As a couple they continued to do what they could to make a difference in their world.

I met the Samontes while speaking at a college missions retreat in Manila. As we became acquainted, Deng confided his growing concern for the safety of his family in Manila. Though martial law had changed the political environment, Deng was remembered for his work in Tondo—and his radical leftist influences. It was the kind of record that the special martial law police would take an active interest in. There was good reason to be concerned.

As the young couple shared their fears with me, I suggested that it might be prudent to consider serving the poor in Christ's name in some country other than their homeland. When I told them about the challenge of Bangladesh and the desperate need of those impoverished people, my burden became theirs. Coupled with a recognition of the great spiritual needs of that Muslim country, the burden became a call. In a matter of months they were off to Bangladesh.

Deng put his engineering and community organizational skills to good use in Dhaka. He served first as a building consultant for HEED, a Christian relief and development consortium, and then as project director for World Vision's impressive community development program. This was a program designed to assist several thousand desperately poor villagers who, dislocated by war, had been "dumped" with no resources on an island in the river system flowing through Dhaka.

There, Deng organized the people for action. The community was improved, jobs were created, children received needed

medical care, mothers were trained in nutrition, health, and pre-
ventative medicine. More important, the people developed a
feeling of dignity, of self-worth. Now they were able to exercise
some control over their lives.

Sucel used her marketing and personnel skills in a local
handicraft program. And together they regularly taught Bible
studies in their home. These studies, along with their personal
witness, caused many Muslim friends to open their lives to
Jesus Christ.

Deng and Sucel are still serving together, now back in
their homeland where Deng serves as a consultant in community
development activities with Conservative Baptists and World
Vision. Their concern for both the social and spiritual needs of
men and women has found an effective expression in their
shared life of service to others.

Just one young couple. One man and one woman with a
heart for the poor . . . and the One who comes to them in the
poor. What a difference they are making! Government programs can move mountains, but only compassionate servants of
Jesus Christ can change a human heart. Ask the people of
Dhaka. They saw more than a caring, dedicated couple. They
saw the face of God.

PART 2

"Let us not become weary in doing good, for at the proper time we will reap a harvest if we do not give up. Therefore, as we have opportunity, let us do good to all people, especially to those who belong to the family of believers" **(Galatians 6:9, 10).**

"I have come that they may have life, and have it to the full" (John 10:10).

Chapter 5

The Mandate for Development

I was six years old, a first grader. For weeks my teacher and my mother had prepared me for my first thespian performance. The appointed day had come. My mother and grandmother arrived early to claim front row seats in the primary school auditorium. My older sister and brother were there—their classes had been dismissed to attend the First Class Play. Even my father had taken off work early so he could attend.

There were only six words to my line in the play. I had memorized them and rehearsed them for days. My performance was hugely important to me . . . the class was counting on me, and even more important, I just couldn't let the family down!

I awaited my cue, standing nervously in the darkened wings of the stage. At last it came, and I entered, stage right. Somehow it seemed different from what I'd anticipated. I couldn't see any audience at first—but I could hear them—feel them—out there in the blackness. And those lights—they were blinding! It took several long minutes for my eyes to adjust . . . faces . . . *waiting* faces. They were waiting to hear me open my mouth and speak!

I heard the teacher clear her throat. I heard her whisper

83

urgently for me to begin. I opened my mouth and—silence! Not one word would come forth. Not one word (remember, there were six!) could I remember. In fright and humiliation I fled the stage.

Let's stop right here. I remember that I was first aware that I might have a problem while I was still waiting in the wings. You could call it a *physical* problem. A strange, uneasy, unsettled feeling in the pit of my stomach. I was first aware of an *emotional* problem as I stood in the hot glare of the stage lights and peered out into the audience in search of a friendly face. And did I ever have an *intellectual* problem! I couldn't remember a single word. Finding shelter in the darkness backstage, I wept over my failure. I was ashamed. I had humiliated my family. I was a failure. This was a real *spiritual* crisis. Why, at that moment of time I felt absolutely without worth. Not even God could love me!

Obviously I've never forgotten that crisis. Although it seems trivial in comparison to some of the things I've faced in my adult life, it underlines a major truth I've encountered again and again. The lesson is this: Life cannot be divided up into neat little packages of

physical,
emotional,
intellectual,
and
spiritual.

Our world doesn't break into finely-drawn segments of

social,
political,
economic,
and
religious.

Whether we recognize it or not, there is an *integration* in life which brings all of the various parts and experiences together into a single entity, an entity which may reflect either wholeness or brokenness.

I once heard Billy Graham say that his wife Ruth had pinned a sign on the window curtain above her kitchen sink. It read: *Divine Services Performed Here Daily!*

Now that's integration! Discovering that there is no distinction between the sacred and the secular. To the Christian, all of life and its experiences are sacred. All too often we try to divide up life like a pie.

But this is a false image of life. Far better to diagram our human existence in an integrated fashion, like this:

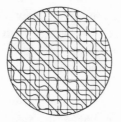

Let the horizontal lines represent the physical and the vertical lines the spiritual. Let those wavy diagonal lines represent the emotional and the straight diagonal lines the intellectual.

Now repeat the diagram and place a large black dot within the circle like this:

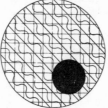

Let this big black dot represent a problem in life, your life. Now what kind of problem do you have? A physical problem? Spiritual? Intellectual? Or is it an emotional problem? Look more closely. You will see that each of the lines intersects at some point within the big black dot. You *do* have a problem!

God created man and woman as whole persons. Sin and failure disrupt and destroy that wholeness, but God comes in Jesus Christ to make us whole again.

OF GHOSTS AND CORPSES

E. Stanley Jones once wrote: "An individual gospel without a social gospel is a soul without a body, and a social gospel without an individual gospel is a body without a soul. One is a ghost and the other is a corpse."

I met someone the other day who had just seen a ghost. Not the familiar kind made by draping mother's bed sheet over the body of a fantasizing child. A real ghost! Or at least that's the way it appeared.

I met this person in a small alleyway in one of the poorest districts in the ancient city of Dhaka. With a Bible tucked under one arm and a "God loves you" pin fastened to his coat collar, he was walking through the filthy, smelly alley "doing the work of the Kingdom."

I stood back in the shadows and watched. An emaciated mother with three filthy kids at her side was carefully picking through the garbage. Maybe there was a scrap of food worth offering the hungriest of her three children. The youngsters' round, hollow eyes looked on, hopefully and hungrily.

At that point, our man-with-the-Bible moved into action. With practiced speed he pulled out a pamphlet from between the covers of his Bible. It was not a coupon to purchase food at a local eatery, however. It was a gospel tract.

I couldn't see whether the tract was in English or translated into Bengali. It wasn't important. The artwork on the cover told me the contents. I had seen it so often before in similar circumstances. The first words were *"God loves you and has a wonderful plan for your life!"*

The Bible-toting stranger I had met in the alleyway had seen a ghost; in fact, four of them. For when we see souls to be saved without responding also to bodies which are broken and diseased through malnutrition, we are seeing "souls without bodies."

We're seeing ghosts.

DEVELOPMENT: MAN'S INTERVENTION OR GOD'S TRANSFORMATION

In recent years the Church has become increasingly willing to see real, whole persons—not just ghosts. Many believers are beginning to grapple—some for the very first time—with a biblical understanding of human development. Christian relief and development agencies have proliferated and prospered. Development is being recognized as a legitimate activity of the Church, along with its responsibilities of evangelism, discipling, and church-planting. As these development activities have multiplied, definitions and theologies of development have been formulated.

Working together with theologians and development professionals, World Concern defines Christian development as "a process that enables people to consider, choose, and implement alternatives for their lives that are consistent with God's intention for mankind."

This development process must promote self-reliance in meeting basic individual and community needs; it should progress toward the equitable distribution of human, economic, and material resources; and it should provide each person an opportunity for fuller participation in the economic and political life of his country, providing personal life-experiences which are consistent with God's intentions for humankind.

Bob Moffit, in a paper written for the World Evangelical Fellowship's Wheaton '83 Consultation, defined development as "every biblically-based activity of the Body of Christ, his Church, which assists in bringing men toward the place of complete reconciliation with God and complete reconciliation with their fellow men and their environment."

This is certainly a much more full understanding of development than that which is practiced by secular and governmental bodies—institutions which acknowledge neither the fundamental spirituality of persons nor the destructive force of evil upon all that which God made as good.

Edward Dayton, Vice President for Mission and Evangelism of World Vision International, speaks of development in terms of social transformation. In a paper prepared for the same Consultation, he speaks of an "intentional social transformation . . . a process of external intervention intended to enable the people to become better than they were before."

Before proceeding in our understanding of the term, it may be helpful to distinguish between the words *relief* and *development*. There is an important difference.

In practical terms . . . what does *relief* really mean? Let's consider one dramatic example.

RELIEF: HELP FOR THE HELPLESS

In the middle of the night, a moonless night, a thousand dogs began to bark, whine, and howl. Though dawn was far away, roosters for miles around began to crow like there was no tomorrow. Then people began to awaken from their sleep, sensing an undulation of the earth beneath them—a low, ominous rumbling. And then there was silence. And then all hell broke loose.

A sound like a million freight trains tore through the night, coupled with a wrenching, sickening convulsion of earth, stone, and steel. Walls parted with a scream, streets collapsed into yawning canyons, and ceilings descended in a nightmare of thunder, choking dust, and mingled cries of pain and terror. Whole hillsides rumbled into chasms where there had been no chasms only moments before.

And then again, there was silence . . . the silence of death.

In a matter of a few seconds, 25,000 Guatemalans perished. It was February 4, 1976. And following on the heels of one of the century's most devastating earthquakes, a massive relief effort—without precedent in this hemisphere—began the mind-staggering task of rebuilding shattered lives.

At the very beginning, the most urgent concern was to pull the still-living from the ruins. And then the dead had to be buried—no small assignment in itself. Clean water supplies had to be restored. Hungry, homeless people began to gather in endless food lines. Emergency medical supplies were rushed to makeshift hospitals.

Following the initial surge of emergency help, the second wave of assistance began a few days later—the rebuilding. Tens of thousands of earthquake-blasted homes, shops, churches, and public buildings needed to be repaired—or razed and replaced.

Guatemala—broken and bleeding after that massive '76 earthquake—needed immediate emergency assistance. And that is *relief*. Relief is doing something for somebody who cannot do it for himself. It is crisis intervention, an attempt to provide some form of assistance that will aid an individual or group to return to a prior state or condition.

Normally, one identifies relief with crisis intervention during times of war, famine, natural disasters, or major dislocations of large groups of people. Its assistance is intended to be temporary in nature and limited in scope.

If that is relief, what, then, is development?

DEVELOPMENT: HELPING PEOPLE HELP THEMSELVES

Development has to do with *process* rather than a single event. From a Christian perspective, it helps individuals and groups discover God's intentions for humankind. God does have a plan for life. Development assists people in understanding and articulating their needs. As in relief, development too includes external intervention. In relief, however, this intervention is to provide rescue; in development, it is intended to *enable*. Development assumes that people have the innate skills and abilities to take charge of their lives, while at the same time acknowledges the need for facilitators to provide example, instruction, and access to resources.

When I think of development, my mind returns to a message a World Concern worker in the Philippines received a number of years ago. The message came from a Filipino Christian in a remote rural village. Most of the people in the village were Christians. But they were weary of the oppressive poverty they endured year after year. Part of the year they lived in plenty. The rest of the year they were impoverished.

The development worker went to the distant village and listened carefully as the elders articulated their need.

"If we don't find a way to earn some money to buy food for our families during the off-harvest time of the year, our children will die from hunger or disease."

It is just at this point that the distinction between relief and development becomes clear.

Relief would immediately establish a feeding program in the village. *Development*, on the other hand, would take time to observe, listen, and help the local populace to identify what meager resources they might have—resources which, if properly utilized and focused, might help them solve their *own* problem.

"It's either feast or famine," said one frustrated farmer.

The development worker asked him to explain.

"In the fruit-bearing season we have mangoes, pineapples, and oranges—far more than we can use for our own needs. But the markets are too far distant to sell our surplus to others."

It was true, there were no roads into the village, only seemingly endless mountain paths, narrow and steep.

"The fruit just rots on the ground in April and we are starving in November!"

The worker asked a few careful questions to help the community leaders discover their own solution.

"If we could save April's feast for November's famine," ventured one of the elders, "we would find life so much easier."

And that is just what they did. The solution to their dilemma was to be packaged in attractive jars labeled "Mountain Fresh Jams and Jellies." You can find them on the shelf of any major Manila supermarket and enjoy them on your breakfast toast in several of Manila's finest tourist hotels.

What did it take? First, a heart of compassion and a willingness to listen—really listen. Next, it required a small financial investment and some training and supervision to help the local villagers learn the canning and preserving process. Finally, it took some creative assistance in helping the producers move their product into the metropolitan market place.

And the result? One more group of Christians discovered for themselves the "abundant life" promised to all of God's creation.

Development . . . helping people help themselves . . . allowing men and women the dignity and encouragement of analyzing and solving their own problems.

BACK TO THE GARDEN

The very first page of the Bible assures us that "In the beginning God created the heavens and the earth." After each creative event are the words, "And God saw that it was good." In its original state, life wore the mantle of perfection. There was no need for "development" or transformation, only for faithful stewardship by man and woman of this perfect creation.

> God blessed them and said to them, "Be fruitful and increase in number; fill the earth and subdue it. Rule over the fish of the sea and the birds of the air and over every living creature that moves on the ground."

> Then God said, "I give you every seed-bearing plant on the face of the whole earth and every tree that has fruit with seed in it. They will be yours for food. And to all the beasts of the earth and all the birds of the air and all the creatures that move on the ground—everything that has the breath of life in it— I give every green plant for food." And it was so.
>
> God saw all that he had made, and it was very good. And there was evening, and there was morning—the sixth day (Genesis 1:28-31).

Nothing need be added. God's perfect creation was all the human family needed. But life did not remain in its original perfection and purity.

LOSS OF A HERITAGE

Through the willful disobedience of man and woman, sin entered into the human experience. As a result of this act of disobedience, the human family was separated from God's perfect creation.

For the woman, childbearing would be accomplished only through pain. This pain is representative of all the risk implicit in both childbearing and childrearing. To this very day much social intervention must focus upon the unusual vulnerability of women and children. They are the members of the human family who suffer the consequences of hunger, disease, and poverty the most.

Man's lot was one of painful toil because of the curse upon the ground. Thorns and thistles crowded out the lush, life-giving vegetation of the perfect creation. Basic food needs from that day forward would become associated with toil, sweat, disappointment, and difficulty.

Finally, death—the ultimate indignity—would reach its malevolent tentacles into every aspect of man and woman's existence. And so it is. Daily newspapers chronicle the unmistakable marks of death and dying in our cultures, civilizations, and environment. And so the human stage is set for the need of development, for the need of spiritual and social transformation.

LIFE MUST GO ON

Adam and Eve—and their seed—separated now from God's perfect creation, discover that life must go on. Toil and sweat, pain, sorrow, and death become endemic to humankind's existence.

The blessings of creation and the multiplication of the human family continue to operate, even as God promised. But the mixture of blessing and curse is unmistakable. Abel is murdered by his brother Cain. In judgment the Lord tells Cain that "when you work the ground, it will no longer yield its crops for you. You will be a restless wanderer on the earth" (Genesis 4:12). The fruit of that curse afflicts all of humankind even to this day. Famines, pestilence, droughts, and floods grip the face of the whole planet. Refugee groups numbering in the millions, wanderers on the earth, seek shelter, food, and security. The need for intervention, transformation, and development couldn't be clearer.

There's good news along with the bad news, however. God has invested his creation with certain gifts: gifts of intelligence, creativity, artistic and mechanical skills . . . and an innate will to survive. Those early, wandering descendants of Adam and Eve became builders of cities (Genesis 4:17), animal herders (Genesis 4:20), skilled metallurgists, and tool makers (Genesis 4:22). Humankind was not left without resources. They possessed the creative and intellectual resources needed to develop the natural resources God had so generously provided in creation.

So human history moves forward. Generations of descendants from Seth to Lamech toiled in the sun, extended human intelligence and creativity, and learned to develop the land and resources.

Lamech had a notable son named Noah. We remember Noah, of course, for his faithfulness to God and his accomplishments in building, supplying, and occupying the ark. But have you ever thought of him as the first development specialist? It was said of Noah: "He will comfort us in the labor and painful toil of our hands caused by the ground the Lord has cursed" (Genesis 5:29). That's an accurate description of a development professional!

A Refugee Moves into Development

Had there been an *Ur of the Chaldees Chronicle* in Abram's day, one of its morning headlines might have read, PROMINENT CITIZEN LEAVES ALL FOR LIFE OF DESERT NOMAD! It surely made little sense to Abram's friends and neighbors. But the Lord God had appeared to Abram with an unmistakable call: "Leave your country, your people and your father's household and go to the land I will show you" (Genesis 12:1).

To Abram's neighbors, the move might have been a mere oddity—the kind of curiosity piece you might read about in the morning newspaper, frown, shake your head, and then go on to the sports page.

But it was more—so much more than that. For the God of all creation sent Abram on his journey with an awesome promise ringing in his ears:

> "I will make you into a great nation
>   and I will bless you;
> I will make your name great,
>   and you will be a blessing.
> I will bless those who bless you,
>   and whoever curses you I will curse;
> and all peoples on earth
>   will be blessed through you"
>   (Genesis 12:2, 3).

Later, God spoke again: "To your offspring I will give this land. . . . To your descendants I give this land, from the river of Egypt to the great river, the Euphrates" (Genesis 12:7, 15:18).

And still later, upon the occasion that God changed this man's name to Abraham, the Lord confirmed his covenant yet again: "As for me, this is my covenant with you: You will be the father of many nations. . . . I will make you very fruitful; I will make nations of you, and kings will come from you" (Genesis 17:4, 6).

Then after years of barrenness on the part of Sarah, Abraham's wife, God completes the vow to Abraham by promising a son, a son to be born in Abraham's one-hundredth year of life, his wife's ninetieth year.

A SPECIAL MEANING TO THE PROMISE

These promises to Abraham are usually considered for their historical importance. They help us understand the foundations of the Jewish nation. Yet the implications of this passage run much deeper than that . . . touching the redemption of the entire human race.

Jesus spoke of Abraham's significance. And the apostle Paul, in his letter to the Christians at Rome, emphasized that "Abraham believed God, and it was credited to him as righteousness" (Romans 4:3).

As a result of this faith, Abraham became the father of many nations, just as it had been promised. An understanding of the significance of Abraham in God's redemptive plan is furthered in the Book of Galatians:

> Consider Abraham: "He believed God, and it was credited to him as righteousness." Understand, then, that those who believe are children of Abraham. The Scripture foresaw that God would justify the Gentiles by faith, and announced the gospel in advance to Abraham: "All nations will be blessed through you." So those who have faith are blessed along with Abraham, the man of faith (Galatians 3:6-9).

FOUNDATIONS FOR DEVELOPMENT

Not diminishing in any way Abraham's importance as the father of the Jewish people or his very special importance in God's redemptive history, let's take a moment to see the patriarch of faith in relation to a biblical understanding of development. God was now promising that what had been lost through Adam and Eve's sin in the Garden would be regained through Abraham and his seed.

God created man and woman complete, in wholeness. Sin had destroyed that wholeness. But God's passionate desire for humankind's wholeness has not changed. God's concern for this wholeness is reflected in the covenant promises he made to Abraham and to his descendants. These promises reach over vast periods of time and through Abraham and his descendants affect all nations.

If God has provided in creation all that is necessary for life, what are the principles we need to learn to help us achieve that life?

ONE: A PROMISED RELATIONSHIP BETWEEN MAN AND GOD

Without the promise of a relationship between God and man, life has no order. There is no purpose or meaning. It is at this very point there is such a fundamental difference between a secular view of development and a biblical understanding.

Tom Sine, historian and futures consultant to several Christian relief and development agencies, notes that western secular views of development are "based on the implicit belief that society is inevitably progressing toward the attainment of a temporary materialistic kingdom. Unending economic and social progress is a natural condition of free persons."

This idea of progress is a cornerstone of the secular religion of the western world. Sine further notes: "Not only was the Creator seen as passive, but His creation was also seen as a passive realm, a grab bag of physical resources available for the taking. This dualistic view of God and His universe has resulted in a desacralization of His creation, *freed from the purposes and presence of God*. Westerners learned to think of the world around them as nothing but passive resources to be exploited to enable them to achieve their materialistic dreams for the future."

This same kind of thinking has led to the despoiling of the earth, the waste and misuse of its resources, the pollution of the environment, and the oppression of large groups of people, while the earth's resources are used to benefit a small minority of earth's population.

Development must begin with a clear understanding of the creative order and of a Creator, a God who has revealed himself and who promises his creation a personal relationship with himself. God spoke in very personal terms to Abraham. His promises were specific and direct. He called Abraham to "walk before me and be blameless." God is recognized as the One whom "I have now seen [and] the one who sees me."

The sense of relationship and participation between the Creator and his creation is evident in many primitive cultures unspoiled by western secular thought. While he does not understand it in Christian terms, the primitive farmer understands the direct relationship between plowing, planting, cultivating, and the gods of the harvest. Our Christian message gives content, clarity, and definition to these primitive beliefs. To separate the God of creation from development—to secularize life and human toil—is to cast aside all order, to remove purpose and meaning from our existence.

I have observed an interesting phenomenon again and again as I've worked with new Christians in the third world. Unspoiled by the excesses and affluence of our rich Western cultures, these dear believers seem to respond naturally to the needs of their own families and communities as a direct response to their newly discovered relationship with God. A level of poverty that was once considered appropriate is no longer acceptable.

Hear their voices:

"Help us make our lives a little better . . ."

"We want our children to have an education . . ."

"Can you open a clinic to help us when we are sick?"

"We want to build a little chapel where we can meet together for worship, but we have no money. Can you help us?"

Are these crass requests for handouts? Not at all. When a person enters into a special relationship with God, his expectations for life increase. And with the increased expectations comes an increased eagerness to "do something" about making life better, more ordered, less oppressive.

Development, then, must begin with the promised relationship between God and man. Development schemes which ignore this fundamental truth will ultimately fail. Earlier, in our definition of development, we noted that development implies *intervention*. God himself intervened in the beginning when the earth was "without form and void." The creative days that followed are evidence of his intervention. The succeeding centuries of history recorded in the book of Genesis confirm that there must be a continuation of that intervention in order to change the course, to turn back the decay and destruction. That intervention begins with God's personal relationship with man. Then God chooses to use men and women for that continuity of intervention. Abraham is God's witness to this truth.

Two: A Promised Relationship between Man and His Seed

The Lord called Abraham aside and said, "Look at the heavens and count the stars—if indeed you can count them. . . . So shall your offspring be" (Genesis 15:5).

Life must go on. Without seed, without descendants, there is no continuity to life. God's developmental purposes are made plain to Abraham by promising him descendants and the protection of that seed.

Poverty, disease, hunger, war, and oppression combine to assault this divine promise of posterity. All the forces of human need attack the promise and attempt to destroy it. It was so in Abraham's day and it is so today.

In a country like Bangladesh, where one out of every four children die before they reach age five, and a second child dies before reaching the teen years, we can begin to understand how this divine promise continually hangs by a thread.

Whereas infant mortality rates in the first year of a child's life in the United States are 12 deaths per 1,000 (and in some western nations they are as low as 7 per 1,000), in the poorest countries of the world more than 150 out of every 1,000 children die before reaching their first birthday. In these same countries, annual average income is more than *fourteen times* less than in the United States.

There is a direct relationship between these statistics. All development programs must give priority to the problems of infant mortality and childhood disease.

But wait. Let us again remind ourselves that these cold statistics wear human faces. Let me take you back to Calcutta for a moment, to a large old house at the end of a dusty road on the outskirts of the city. Just over the walled-in yard of the house, a huge urban slum squats, its squalor and smells constantly reminding the nearby homes of its presence.

Mrs. Banarjee had invited me to see her home for abandoned children and to inspect some of the handiwork of the Women's Welfare Society. Eighteen darling children greeted me with their polite "Namiste" and sang songs they had learned, in heavily accented English as well as in Hindi. Their eager faces and smiling eyes more than compensated for some of the discordant sounds coming from their untrained voices.

I listened carefully to their stories. Mrs. Banarjee told me about a family of three children left on the doorstep of the home. These little ones had been abandoned by a father left widowed without any resources to care for his children while he tried to earn a few rupees each day as an independent carpenter. His "shop" was a busy Calcutta sidewalk, his home a three-foot-high shack made of sticks, cardboard, and mud. A six-month-old infant was being tenderly cared for by her substitute mother, an eight-year-old sister! She was fully responsible to try to keep together the three kids, now her only family. Here in Mrs. Banarjee's home she found food and shelter, love and learning, and the care needed to survive.

Rajah, a robust six-year-old, had been "donated" to the home. His mother had no alternative. There were five children in the home and scarcely enough food for three. Rajah seemed best prepared to care for himself, and this might give her the chance to stretch the food enough to care for the other four.

Then there was "Miriam." I nicknamed her so because she tended her brother with all the care I would have expected from the sister of Moses. She is all her brother has left. Father deserted the home; he could stand no longer the guilt and despair he felt in seeing his family suffer. Two of his children had already died from hunger. Mother returned to her family in a distant village. But there was no food there for three. She hoped her placement of her surviving children in Mrs. Banarjee's home would be temporary. She knew when she left them, however, that she might never see them again.

Choices! Terrible choices! Did these Calcutta mothers love their children less than a mother in Chicago? Do they feel the pain of their separation any less than we? What must the pain and despair feel like for a father who has *no* possible resources adequate to care for his family?

Choices! Choices no human being should have to make. Choices which violate God's special relationship between man and his seed.

THREE: A PROMISED RELATIONSHIP BETWEEN MAN AND LAND

Life must have meaning, purpose. For this need, God promises a relationship between man and himself. Life must have continuity. For this need, God promises seed. Life must have the necessary resources to function and grow. For this need, God promises land.

"To your descendants I give this land" (Genesis 15:18).

In chapter 3 I spoke of the need for man to control the land he farms in order to have control over his life and future. Land is representative of all the various resources God has provided his creation. These resources must be developed in order for humankind to prosper. And each person must have *access* to these resources or he will be controlled by others.

Consider the plight of the slum-dwellers in Colombo's "Hell's Seventeen Acres." Their squatter shacks along the national highway had been bulldozed by government road crews in order to beautify the roadway from the international airport to the city . . . preparation made for the arriving delegates to a third world conference on poverty!

Or think of the poor Manobo tribesmen in the Philippines. They lived in a culture more geared to the sixteenth century than the twentieth. Their fathers and grandfathers had farmed the jungle-forested mountainsides for generations. National "development" schemes brought tens of thousands of lowlanders to the island of Mindanao to develop a food growing industry— pineapples, tomatoes, bananas—for export markets where tables were already overflowing with food. And the powerless tribal people were pushed off their ancestral lands, farther and farther into the jungles, where even subsistence farming was impossible.

It is interesting to note that in the beginning God the Creator gave man and woman their place in the sun—"a garden in the east, in Eden." When Satan called Adam and Eve to leave their life of obedience to God, they did not then understand that the consequence of their disobedience would be the loss of their heritage of land in Eden. And in this act of disobedience, the world's first refugee problem was created. In Abraham, however, the promise of land ownership is restored, and with the rights to the land come control over its resources. Individual access to resources is a fundamental principle of development.

God renews this promise of land to Moses at Sinai. Sinai stands between Egypt and the Promised Land not only geographically, but also symbolically. Egypt represents oppression and bondage, a time when Israel had no resources, no land, no control over their future. The Promised Land was a land with the promise of abundance, a place where men and women could live in peace with the resources and capacity to control their destinies. Sinai symbolizes Law and Order, the place where God articulates the principles (development principles) necessary in order for men and women to move from oppression—Egypt—to abundance—the Promised Land.

It *always* requires a journey, a process, an intervention to move from bondage to abundance. That journey is one of discovering the order of creation—the will and way of God. This process, this journey, we call development.

People become oppressed. Land and resources are taken from them. The result: Their posterity—their seed—is threatened. They can no longer depend upon themselves. The people cry out. In their distress they plead for help. God hears the people's cry. He remembers his covenant, and he calls humankind into these special relationships.

These, then, are the foundation stones for development. The development process, engaged in from a biblical perspective, is that process which has the potential to move people from oppression to abundance.

GOD'S EXCHANGE SYSTEM

Development brings people together, keeps them working together, and enables them to share the resources and benefits of their particular environment. In this process, oppression and injustice are restrained, a spirit of hope and trust is encouraged, and life takes on meaning where there has been only emptiness and despair.

Those who understand development understand the fundamental principle that *all* people of the earth possess *both* needs and resources. In the affluent West, we think in terms of our possessing *resources* to meet the *needs* of impoverished third world peoples. But we *all* have resources, we all have needs. Development, then, is that exchange system which facilitates the transfer of adequate resources to meet appropriate needs.

Haitian farmers profit by assistance in farming techniques, animal husbandry improvements, and resource management to help them meet their need for food to feed their families. Poor Christian Haitian families, on the other hand, possess very special family values that busy, over-committed, wildly independent families in our affluent cities and farms can profit from.

Each group has needs. Each has resources.

Development engaged in from a biblical perspective will help distribute both the needs and resources so that all involved in the process can live more whole and fulfilling lives . . . the kind of lives our loving Creator intends for his creation.

"For although they knew God, they neither glorified him as God nor gave thanks to him, but their thinking became futile and their foolish hearts were darkened. . . . They exchanged the truth of God for a lie, and worshiped and served created things rather than the Creator" (Romans 1:21, 25).

"For what I do is not the good I want to do; no, the evil I do not want to do—this I keep on doing. . . . What a wretched man I am! Who will rescue me . . . ?"
(Romans 7:19, 24).

Chapter 6

The Problem of Evil

A wave of dread swept through me when I saw the suitcase. In his haste, our houseboy, Aning, had left it in his room. He was hurrying home on an inter-island steamer to Samar, four hundred miles from our home in Manila. I knew his boat was set to leave within the hour, at midnight. From the North Port.

Situated in the very heart of Tondo, the city's most crowded section, completely encircled by the city's worst slums, Manila's infamous North Port was a place dreaded by foreigners in broad daylight. Only the brave—or the careless—entered this place of violence at night.

But it had to be done. Aning would need that bag. I had to get it to him—or at least try. I called my dog, an old boxer who looked more fierce than she really was, to accompany me. I'm not sure what security I expected her to bring. Going into Tondo with Duchess for protection was about as effective as fending off a gorilla with a toothbrush.

We had just reached the darkest, most dangerous part of the slum, when my faithful protector chose to become carsick!

Maybe she was just coughing. Maybe she would be all right. Maybe . . . no, she was definitely ill. I stopped the car under the light of one of the few street lamps.

It didn't take me long to realize that my worst fears had been justified. Not only was I a foreigner in Tondo at midnight, I had also managed to arrive at the height of a gang war. With a sick dog. Great!

Several hundred young men were lined up on opposing sides. The "Sigue-Sigue" were out to revenge last night's attack on the "Oxo!" I pulled Duchess back into the car just as the barrage of flying missiles began. The air was suddenly alive with zinging rocks, bottles, and assorted other projectiles fired from huge sling-shots. I rammed my little car into gear and stomped on the throttle—my fright greater than my offense at my dog's indisposition.

WHICH WORLD IS REAL?

Putting distance between the car and the raging street war, my racing heart began to idle down a little. I found myself thinking about all the people—all the men, women, and children—who called this seething slum "home."

The stench rushing in through the open window reminded me that this enormous population center had virtually no sanitation at all. The black windows of its dilapidated shacks stared at me from the narrow streets like the empty eye sockets of a skull. The simile is appropriate. Tondo is a place of death, fear, hunger, and numbing despair.

I couldn't help visualizing some of the glossy tourist brochures. With slick, four-color persuasion, the pamphlets crooned a Manila of "old world charm and new world modernity."

A tourist could believe that. Standing alongside the graceful Manila Hilton or eating in the splendid garden court of one of the city's five-star restaurants or driving down Forbes Park Boulevard with its rows of picturesque, tiled-roof homes, you could almost believe the myth.

You could dine, shop, sight-see, sunbathe, and snap your

Instamatic for days without ever touching the alternate world of bloody street-battles, open sewers, and crushing poverty just a few miles away.

Which world is the real world? Which better represents the reality of the planet we call home? The slick tourist brochures and the high-walled garden terrace of the Hilton . . . or the nightmare called Tondo?

My travels all over the globe have stripped away all doubt. The Tondos are reality for the overwhelming majority of the world's people. To those who are willing to look—or care—they give a clear picture, in microcosm, of what has really gone wrong.

THORNS IN THE GARDEN

What *has* gone wrong?

We started the last chapter by pointing out that God the creator made everything good . . . in the beginning. He saw all that he had made, "and it was very good."

But alas, there are thorns in the garden and thistles in the cabbage patch!

God made man and woman with the capacity for both good and evil, the ability both to distinguish and to choose between right and wrong. This innate ability to choose to do good or to do evil, to obey or to disobey, this ability to make moral decisions is what distinguishes the human family from all the rest of God's creation.

For it is out of this ability to choose that men and women are empowered to love. God loved all he created, and he desired, above all else, that the human lives he created would exercise their ability to choose . . . and love him in return.

This love was first tested by obedience when God placed limitations on man's choices. Adam and his bride were free to enjoy all God had created for their enjoyment and well being. But the fruit of one particular tree was off limits. "You must not eat from the tree of the knowledge of good and evil," the Lord told them, "for when you eat of it you will surely die" (Genesis 2:17).

Just one simple test of obedience . . . which they failed. Deceived by the serpent's seductive offer, they crossed their Creator's loving barrier to eat the fruit of that tree. And so death came into the midst of life. That death, through Adam's sin, has been passed on to all persons in every generation—the original sin that remains at the very root of all earth's problems and sorrows.

Had things remained as they were in the beginning, had our first parents not fallen into sin, there would be no need for a book on the subject of development. A perfect creation needs no development! But through sin perfection was lost. Now sin and death are the dominant reality in our troubled world. Therefore we must learn what it means to help, heal, and restore—in Jesus' name—those who are broken. This book is written with the purpose of assisting each reader to understand development, its biblical foundations, and why each individual Christian as well as every local church should be engaged in the compassionate ministries which feed the hungry, heal the sick, shelter the homeless, and liberate the oppressed.

WHAT GOD JOINED TOGETHER, MAN PULLED ASUNDER

"People are the problem!"

That was the frustrated retort of one community development worker who in youthful idealism had come to a desperately poor people in a depressed third world country in order to help lift them from their misery. But his perfect development schemes just wouldn't work because people kept messing things up!

What school teacher hasn't felt that same frustration when Johnny won't learn to read? How many pastors have left the ministry when the people he has come to "lead to righteousness" continue in their self-centered, rebellious ways? The judge and probation officer, the reformer and the revivalist could all sing the same chorus of despair. Evil has a malevolent grip on people's lives—and it doesn't easily let go. It's enough to cause a person to give up!

This chapter begins with a quote from the book of Romans on this very subject. Paul shows how humankind exchanges light for darkness, truth for lie, life for destruction. He also confesses his own struggle with evil. Apart from the saving grace of Jesus Christ, he would despair of it all.

This is a fundamental truth we all need to understand. It is raised to even greater significance when we consider the whole area of social change, human development, and societal transformation. *All human development programs which do not take seriously the sinful nature of man are destined to fail!*

TODAY'S LIBERATORS—TOMORROW'S OPPRESSORS

The Bolsheviks of Czarist Russia developed their revolutionary influence by promising to deliver the oppressed masses from the despotic rule of a whole succession of Czars. A brief encounter with Russian history of the late nineteenth and early twentieth centuries would convince you how much that deliverance was needed. In their zeal to condemn the evil in Russia's ruling class, however, the revolutionaries were blind to their own evil. And the revolution that promised to free the oppressed brought a Communist oppression far greater than the evils they were determined to overthrow. The liberators of the masses became the new oppressors.

One can see this in every human revolutionary movement. Leaders who refuse to acknowledge the evil in their own lives as well as in the lives they are determined to free merely exchange one unjust system for another.

We see the deterioration of these ideals within the history of our own nation. America, born in revolution, is recognized by many struggling third world nations as the primary anti-revolutionary force in society today. Our forefathers overthrew the injustice and oppression of their British masters. But today we find it difficult to relate to new expressions of injustice experienced by today's struggling, impoverished nations. Contemporary King Georges ride roughshod over people with no power, huddled masses who yearn to be free.

Some might feel this is a much too pessimistic view of human history. And while it is true that there are shades and degrees of evil, the principle remains the same: all human development (or freedom) movements which do not take seriously the sinful nature of man are destined to fail.

"AFRICA IS UP FOR GRABS!"

Consider one graphic example within the past generation. Following World War II, a rising tide of nationalism called for the withdrawal of all colonial forces and the establishment of sovereign nations in countries which had been under colonial dominance for decades or centuries.

Nowhere were these voices stronger than in Africa. Opportunistic and charismatic local leaders promised freedom, justice, and economic prosperity. But all too often they did not deliver what was promised. Injustices committed against the people by foreign colonizers were simply replaced by injustices perpetuated by fellow countrymen. Tribalism and religious differences, along with the abuse of power by local and national leaders, continued to make the lives of many citizens of new African nations a difficult existence.

Uhuru! The Swahili call for freedom from European-imposed colonialism brought independence for millions of black Africans, but too often very little liberty. The rallying cry, "One man, one vote," has suffered an ironic distortion. Many Africans gained "one vote," but it can only be cast for one man! There are forty-one major independent Black African nations. Only seven of these allow opposition political parties. Seven are single-party states and seventeen are ruled by the military. In the past twenty-five years, seventy of Africa's political leaders in twenty-nine different countries have been deposed by assassinations, purges, or coups.

While population in the sub-Sahara African countries has increased from 210 million in 1960 to more than 400 million today, foreign debt has escalated to more than $100 billion. The continent is burdened with over five million refugees. Twenty percent of its land has turned into desert, and the process of "desertification" could encompass forty-five percent of Africa within the next fifty years.

One African educational leader summed it up well: "We are undergoing a second colonization. Our present leaders are just like the old tribal chiefs who signed pacts with colonizers for a few beads. Friendship and military pacts are now penciled up in return for guns, aid, or cash loans. Africa is up for grabs!"

British journalist Ian Smiley wrote in the Atlantic Monthly, "Africa is back where it was fifty years ago."

DESTRUCTION OF THE PEARL

Not long ago I flew into Uganda via the Entebbe airport. From the air, the nearby capital city of Kampala had a certain quaint charm about it. As the plane drew up to the deserted terminal, I recalled the Israeli hostage rescue a few years back. The event brought a certain fame to Entebbe—a fittingly bizarre notoriety for a national airport under the control of a mad dictator.

Yawning potholes on the way to my hotel in Kampala made the national road look more like the surface of the moon than a roadway. The signs of decay were unmistakable. Shuttered shops, deserted houses with collapsed roofs, windows without windowpanes. The dusty, rusty gas pumps in an abandoned gasoline station reminded me of a busier life which prevailed in Uganda before the terror of Idi Amin. This "pearl of Africa" was now merely a tarnished remnant of its past.

The hotel lobby was almost deserted. In my room, the suffocating heat bore mute witness to an air conditioning system that hadn't functioned for years. One light bulb burned dimly in a fixture where there was provision for four. Discovering that there was no soap in the bathroom made me thankful I had learned to come prepared with emergency supplies.

That afternoon I took a walk through the shopping area. Most of the shops were closed. Those still open had few goods on their shelves. What was available for purchase was priced beyond the means of all but a few.

I thought of Amin's promise of "plenty" . . . how he was going to "free the land from its colonial past." He succeeded in driving out the colonists, and the land was free—free to be systematically looted and destroyed for the selfish interest of the new power elite.

There is no gain when the self-serving, selfish interest of one group of leaders is exchanged for that of another set of leaders bent toward the same evil. Today's liberators will become tomorrow's oppressors when leadership does not take seriously the sinful nature of humankind.

THE "GREAT LEAP" . . . THAT GOES NOWHERE

China's Maoist revolution promised the citizens of the world's most populous nation deliverance from the political, economic, and social ills of the past. But revolution was a horror of blood-letting. And when it was over, the abuse continued, this time marked by oppression against the old powerful who were now out of power. As the years went by, this new "People's Republic" almost destroyed itself by the "Great Leap Forward" of the 1950s and the "Cultural Revolution" and its Red Guard fanatics during the 1960s.

This is not to discount the good that comes from freedom movements—and even certain revolutions. The point, once again, is simply this: Until human leadership takes seriously the flawed, sinful nature of man and woman, the corrective actions leadership sponsors to correct human behavior will only lend themselves, given enough time, to a whole new set of abuses. This is true whether the revolutionary forces represent the right or the left, the socialist system or the capitalist system.

Apart from an acknowledgment of humankind's fundamental sinfulness, and apart from the redemptive influence of the gospel, well-meaning actions intended to bring liberation will ultimately bring a new oppression which replaces the oppression of the old order.

GOING IN CIRCLES

The western mind is conditioned to think of human history as a linear progression, ever leading forward and upward. Classical liberalism promulgates this view of man's history. It promises to bring in the Kingdom of God through man's efforts.

"Every day in every way the world is getting better and better." Speak this often enough, loud enough, and with enough enthusiasm and belief and it will happen.

Not so! The most cursory examination of contemporary history will belie this promise.

However, an opposite view of human history that sees only human failure and deterioration is, in my opinion, an equally distorted view. This theological viewpoint resigns itself to the inevitability of the progress of evil, saying that all of civilization is "going to hell in a handbasket!"

Both of these viewpoints are flawed by the same misunderstanding and interpretation of human history, that is, that history is a linear progression, either upward or downward.

A more accurate and realistic view of human history will see its ebb and flow, the rise and fall and rise again of both good and evil. The eastern mind is much more conditioned to understanding the cyclical nature of life. Viewing history from this perspective, we must guard against the intrusion of evil at every point. We can also anticipate the good to manifest itself in like manner. The apostle Paul had this understanding of life. On the one hand he complained, "What I do is not the good I want to do

. . ." (Romans 7:19). But at the same time he was able to celebrate a victory—a victory that swept him into the heights of exultation as he both acknowledged his sinfulness and placed himself under the sheltering authority of Jesus Christ. "Who will rescue me from this body of death? Thanks be to God—through Jesus Christ our Lord!" (Romans 7:24-25). Paul had both a realistic understanding of himself and a healthy appreciation for the power of Christ manifest in him.

THE ENEMY IS ME!

All this points to one crucial truth: In any activity intended to facilitate human development, if there is not an acknowledgment of the presence of evil in our world coupled with an appreciation of man's ability to do both good and evil, then such activities will fail; they will founder on the rocky shoals of their own sinful perspectives.

Every development worker engaged in activities intended to benefit the poor, the homeless, and the oppressed, knows all too well the disappointment and disillusionment that comes when these programs self-destruct. In a land reform program where land is distributed to farmers without the resources to develop it, all too often those farmers lose the land to a new set of owners who do control those resources. That farmer was better off as a tenant, working the land his father and grandfather had worked before him, for the landowner often had a historical link with the family which expressed itself in a certain beneficence. The new landowner, on the other hand, with few or no links to the farmer, is coldly indifferent to his needs.

In areas where Christian development agencies are working with large refugee populations, it is essential to work cooperatively with the host government and other assisting governments, along with The United Nations High Commission on Refugees, to help these refugees. In the early days of a major movement of refugees, this works—people are helped.

Then evil begins to surface.

Local government leaders use the refugee program, with its large flow of money and material resources, as an opportunity to enrich themselves, oftentimes to the detriment of the homeless ones. All too often, when the program continues over a long period of time, the selfish interests of government workers become better served than the refugees. Or bureaucracy takes over and the refugee programs become a means of employment for a swelling number of paid workers. The bureaucrats then enforce an escalating number of rules and regulations designed to benefit the needs of the government—rather than the needs of the refugees the program was originally planned to benefit. And it is not unusual for "donor" nations to use their humanitarian assistance as a tool of self-interest to promote their own foreign policy agendas.

Become a Vietnamese boat person in a southeast Asian refugee center for a day. You will experience the frustration and sense of powerlessness they feel while living in a "camp" administered by others. How hard they try to work the only system available to them to get some First World country to sponsor them as refugee immigrants.

I have seen the problems, felt the frustration and pain of young men in Pulau Bidong camp in Malaysia. Some have been in the camp for *years*. They are labeled "unaccompanied minors." With no families either in the camp or in countries to which they are attempting to migrate, they fill out forms, submit to innumerable interviews, and plead their case before several government delegations, only to have all their efforts meet with failure. And hundreds of them still wait!

Hospitals that started in order to bring medical help to the poor all too often end up serving primarily the rich. Examine the patient records of third-world mission hospitals where administrators are caught in a crossfire between the demands from the poor who so desperately need the medical care, and a mission board or sponsoring organization which insists on cutting operational subsidies.

Visit an economic development program where a group of

local businessmen have been provided start-up funding to establish a business which will benefit a large number of workers. The idea is a good one. Invest the capital in a responsible few so the investment can be wisely managed in order to benefit many. But all too often the "trickle-down theory" of investment fails. Selfish interests at the top tend to control profits so that little financial benefit trickles down to help those who need that help so much. The examples are innumerable!

FOR GOOD PEOPLE TO DO NOTHING

We have devoted considerable attention to the active presence of evil in our world, evil people committing evil acts. But Edmund Burke once wrote, "The only thing necessary for the triumph of evil is for good men to do nothing." More than half of the world is living in miserable conditions, half of these in conditions approaching absolute poverty. Food is inadequate. Disease is rampant. Economic opportunity is non-existent. *To do nothing positive with the resources we possess is to commit ourselves to the triumph of evil. To do nothing in the face of evil is to become part of that evil.*

GOD'S CONCERN FOR JUSTICE

We learn, therefore, that evil expresses its presence in the form of oppression of the powerless by the powerful. The Scriptures bear powerful witness of God's concern for justice, his condemnation of all injustice. He tells the prophet Amos, "Let justice roll on like a river, righteousness like a never-failing flood" (Amos 5:24). This call for justice comes after the Lord exposes to the prophet the prevailing forms of injustice abroad in the land.

The neighbors of Israel were spoilers of the land who "threshed Gilead with sledges having iron teeth" (Amos 1:3); they were oppressors who "took captive whole communities and sold them to Edom" (1:6); they disregarded treaties (1:9) and stifled all compassion (1:11).

Then the divine judgment turned toward Israel itself. They too were guilty of unjust deeds committed against the people. You "sell the righteous for silver," declared the Lord. (Remember the silver deals of the Hunt brothers of Texas just a few years ago? Their attempt to control the silver market for their own personal gain caused silver-influenced prices to escalate, then brought financial ruin to many silver investors.)

Israel sells "the needy for a pair of sandals. They trample on the heads of the poor . . . and deny justice to the oppressed" (Amos 2:6,7).

The prophet Amos continues to give the word of the Lord concerning Israel's unjust ways: "You who turn justice into bitterness . . . you hate the one who reproves in court and despise him who tells the truth. You trample on the poor and force him to give you grain. . . . You oppress the righteous and take bribes and you deprive the poor of justice in the courts" (Amos 5:7, 10, 12).

No wonder a holy God calls forth a flood of justice! And the poor of our day, whether they live in an impoverished third world country or in a resource-rich developed country, suffer the same kinds of injustices today.

Until the people of God correct their unjust behavior, God's word to them is:

> I despise your religious feasts;
>   I cannot stand your assemblies.
> Even though you bring me burnt offerings
>   and grain offerings
>   I will not accept them.
> Away with the noise of your songs!
>   I will not listen to the music of your harps.
> But let JUSTICE roll on like a river,
> righteousness like a never-failing stream!
>   (Amos 5:21-24).

Our world would profit more if it had fewer consultations and conventions, fewer congresses and assemblies, and more times of repentance when believer and unbeliever, individual and institution, would seek out all forms of injustice, renounce evil, and commit to expressions of justice which would impact all people.

"Righteousness and justice are the foundation" of God's throne (Psalm 89:14). "Blessed are they who maintain justice, who constantly do what is right (Psalm 106:3). "The Lord loves the just and will not forsake his faithful ones" (Psalm 37:28).

Isaiah warned the people of God that they were guilty of oppressing the fatherless and the widows (1:17), and in their unjust practices were grinding the face of the poor (3:15). The prophet Micah noted that there were two sins which always went together—idolatry and the oppression of the poor. When any group of individuals—or any nation—allows systems to develop which victimize and oppress the poor while making justice serve only the needs and aims of the powerful, that group or nation is sowing the seeds of its own destruction. Writes Walter Brueggeman: "Being in the land without caring for community ends history."

The sins which brought the destruction of Sodom were not those we usually associate with Sodom's abrupt demise. Their sexual impurity and perversions were only symptomatic of their greater sins. Sodom was "arrogant, overfed and unconcerned; they did not help the poor and needy. They were haughty and did detestable things before me. Therefore I did away with them as you have seen" (Ezekiel 16:49).

SYMPTOMS OF SICKNESS IN SOCIETY

We need to pause here and consider our own sins as a people. Though justice is referred to more than three hundred times in Scripture, and the sins of injustice are thoroughly denounced by a righteous God, American evangelicals all too often seem amazingly uncomfortable with the very word . . . *justice*.

Mention it and you sometimes are thought of as a leftist, a theological liberal, or a revolutionary! Perhaps this results from our obsession with material wealth, our uninformed or unrealistic views concerning the broad reach of human poverty, and the possibility that our affluent, consumptive life styles may have some relationship to the poverty of others.

Can a small minority of earth's people control and use a vast majority of the resources and consider itself just?

Can we as a nation continue to consume 140 percent of our daily food needs while large numbers of the earth's people have less than 75 percent of their daily food needs supplied?

We worry about diet and exercise while half of the world's family are concerned with hunger and debilitating disease!

There is something fundamentally unjust with a food distribution system among the world's people which allows this type of imbalance to continue.

As a nation we often pride ourselves on how much we give to the poor. Not diminishing the good we do contribute as a nation, we need to look at the facts a little more closely. In the face of enormous world need, in the face of desperate conditions of poverty and disease which prevail across the globe, we must acknowledge with disappointment that American contribution to the poor ranks *fifteenth* among the developed industrialized nations' official development assistance. Last year our contribution amounted to just a little over one quarter of one percent of our gross national product. Expenditures for national defense were twenty-five times that much!

When one takes into account that more than fifty percent of every foreign assistance dollar we grant returns immediately to the American economy through purchase of American goods and servicing of past debt, the scandal of our national priorities increases.

In a world of such great need, our national security may be far more dependent upon how we respond to the needs of the poor than on the strength of our armies and armaments.

The writer of the book of Proverbs tells us that "Evil men do not understand justice, but those who seek the Lord understand it fully" (Proverbs 28:5). "The righteous care about justice for the poor, but the wicked have no such concern. . . . Whoever is kind to the needy honors God. . . . Speak up and judge fairly; defend the rights of the poor and needy" (Proverbs 29:7; 14:31; 31:9). "Do not exploit the poor because they are poor and do not crush the needy in court. . . . He who despises his neighbor sins, but blessed is he who is kind to the needy. . . . A generous man will himself be blessed, for he shares his food with the poor" (Proverbs 22:22; 14:21; 22:9).

WHO SHALL DELIVER ME FROM THIS EVIL?

Looking straight into the face of evil is not pleasant.

But the presence of evil is real and must be recognized, else we shall fail in all we undertake in alleviating human suffering.

The apostle Paul, recognizing the presence of evil both in the world and in himself, asked a question about deliverance and then answered his own question with an expression of praise: "Thanks be to God—through Jesus Christ our Lord!" Paul understood the triumph over evil when Christ, "in His own body bore our sins on the tree." He understood the triumph over evil which was implicit in Christ's victory over death at resurrection.

"Thanks be to God! He gives us the victory through our Lord Jesus Christ" (1 Corinthians 15:57). Paul expressed that victory daily as he was empowered for living through the indwelling presence of the Holy Spirit. And with the apostle John, he no doubt looked forward to that future and final triumph over evil when there will be "no more death or mourning or crying or pain . . ." (Revelation 21:4). For God himself, wiping every tear from the eyes of those who suffer, will establish a new kingdom of righteousness and the old order of things will pass away.

Without a clear understanding of evil in our world, all activity focused on human development will ultimately fail. Today's liberators will become tomorrow's oppressors. For these very reasons, concerned Christians must not entrust the important work of human development to governments and secular institutions.

We have the spiritual enlightenment, the physical resources, and the redeemed community to go forth into a world crushed by oppression, broken by poverty and suffering, diseased and dying, and do something significant and lasting in meeting these needs.

> If you spend yourselves in behalf of the hungry
> and satisfy the needs of the oppressed,
> then your light will rise in the darkness,
> and your night will become like the noonday.

> The Lord will guide you always;
> he will satisfy your needs in a sun-
> scorched land
> and will strengthen your frame . . .
> you will be called Repairer of Broken Walls,
> Restorer of Streets with Dwellings
> (Isaiah 58:10-12).

"For the kingdom of God is not a matter of eating and drinking, but of righteousness, peace and joy in the Holy Spirit" (Romans 14:17).

Chapter 7

The Kingdom of God

The tropical sun was at its peak of noonday intensity, and the humid air lay heavy with the putrid smell of decaying refuse. I struggled to climb to the top of "Garbage Mountain," a mound of waste as tall as a ten-story building.

I could scarcely believe what I was seeing.

This was Manila, home to me and my family for almost ten years . . . the famed "pearl of the Orient" . . . the Philippines' crown jewel. I knew its many faces. I had lived in its suburbs, shopped in its markets, worshiped in its churches, explored the narrow, twisted alleys of its old Spanish sector, and bargained for "best price" in the many shops of its Chinatown. Manila's parks had been the playground for my growing children. Its U.S. Embassy compound had been a little corner of America the homesick expatriate could escape to on the Fourth of July.

But this . . . this was a Manila I had never experienced.

For this one-hundred-foot-high garbage dump was merely the centerpiece of a struggling community of more than 4,000 human beings. It was difficult to comprehend that men and women, little boys and girls, could possibly survive in such a degrading and inhumane environment. But it was true. This massive mountain of trash was the very source of life for so many of my neighbors.

All night long the huge diesel-powered trucks disgorged their foul contents gathered from the streets of the huge metropolis. One person's discards, however, became another person's source of livelihood. Here was the home for a whole community of people whose only source of income was the bits of wood, iron, glass, and bone scavenged from each freshly dumped load of refuse.

Babies were born in the cardboard and scrap-tin shanties.

Children played—and were sometimes buried alive—in the endless, crumbling slopes of the garbage mountain.

Old women, bent half-way to the ground, labored long hours in the hot sun to discover some newly delivered "treasure" which could be converted into cash.

Long lines formed at the only water spigot . . . almost a mile away.

A number of men sat hunkered at the base of the mountain. These were the local "toughs"—the gangs that controlled even the waste of the city to assure for themselves their half-share in all that was gathered.

My mind reeled even as I struggled to keep from gagging on the overpowering stench. This was certainly a new face—a dark and depraved face—to the city I had called home for such a long time. It hurt to think that in all of my years of ministry, all of my finely-laid strategies for evangelism and church-planting, had never penetrated this corner of urban hell. Although I knew I served a powerful God, my faith staggered at the seeming impossibility of bringing any light—or doing any good—in an area so twisted by years of evil and neglect.

Manila is only a microcosm of a world-wide pattern. We could speak of Ankara or Abidjan, Cairo or Calcutta, Dhaka or Delhi, New York or Nairobi, Tegucigalpa or Timbuktu. Cities, whether you look at their fair facades of steel and glass or their darker images of violence and poverty, are both a historical reality and a rapidly expanding phenomenon of human civilization.

The city represents man's attempt to organize and control life—to master its systems and develop its potential. Although cities have been a part of civilization since almost the beginning of time, the rapid growth of cities—the urbanization of our world—is a more recent result of the shift from an agricultural to an industrial society. And this shift has taken place in a relatively short span of time.

THE MOVE TO THE CITY

In 1960 there were 115 world cities with a population in excess of one million persons. The majority of these cities were in the industrialized countries. By 1980 this number had increased to 227 cities with the majority of these in the developing third world. Urbanologists predict that this number of one-million-or-more-residents cities will increase to 340 by 1990 and almost 450 by the end of this century.

When we used to think of the world's largest metropolises, cities like London, New York, Paris, and Tokyo came to mind. But these have been outstripped in population by third world cities like Bombay and Calcutta, Cairo and Shanghai, Mexico City and Saõ Paulo. Urbanization of the developing world is recognized as one of the "megatrends" of the day.

Mexico City had reached a population of more than eighteen million by 1984, ranking it as the world's largest. With current trends continuing, it will *double* in another seventeen years! The median age for Mexico City's inhabitants is 14.2 years, in comparison with a median age of 31 in my home city of Seattle. No small wonder, then, that this world's expanding urban population is producing ten Seattle-sized cities every month, and almost all of them in the non-industrialized world. And no wonder that these new urban centers suffer unemployment rates of twenty-five to fifty percent!

CITIES OF PROMISE BECOME CITIES OF DESPAIR

Not many years ago, Saõ Paulo, Brazil, was heralded as a "showcase of urban development." Huge skyscrapers pierced the skyline. Thousands of factories churned out all manner of raw materials and finished goods. Its citizens worshiped in churches designed to accommodate 25,000 persons at a single service!

But Saõ Paulo's golden dream has turned into a vicious nightmare.

Today forty percent of its children suffer from anemia, and twenty-two percent of the children entering its primary schools are victims of advanced malnutrition. Considering the inevitable brain damage malnutrition brings to children, one child study warned that the boys and girls of Saõ Paulo "are growing up partially amputated."

Before the vast population influx into Saõ Paulo, the city's average consumption of beans, the Brazilian diet staple, was 2.5 kilograms monthly per capita. During this decade of "development" this has fallen to 1.5 kilograms, while bread consumption has plummeted from 7.8 to 2.5 kilograms monthly per capita. Where ten years ago a Brazilian worker spent an average of 87 hours laboring in a factory in order to purchase the official minimum basic monthly diet, today that same laborer must work 182 hours to buy exactly the same amount of food. The hopes for a better life in the city have become a hollow mockery for millions of migrating rural peasants.

SLUMS ARE THE GIFT OF THE CITY

Whether it is Calcutta's million street-dwellers, the drug-dazed residents of Kathmandu's narrow alleyways, or the despairing families of Nairobi's Mathari Valley, the city has been unable to produce on its promises of prosperity and social advancement. Today, tens of millions live in human wretchedness in crowded slums.

One of the most tragic features of these blighted areas is their pattern of self-perpetuity. They produce a poverty of spirit that affects family life for generations to come.

Why does the city tend to dehumanize life?

While it promises life, all too often it brings only poverty, sickness, and death. In our attempt to build communities, we end up with alienation. In building our cities of power, fame, and security, we find ourselves increasingly powerless, without human dignity, and struggling to survive in an environment of fear and dread.

FROM COMMUNITY TO CITY TO CHAOS

The Scriptures bring insight into this matter of city building. A careful study can help us understand human development from God's perspective.

Adam's initial sin of disobedience manifested its malignant presence in the offspring of earth's first couple. Cain, a tiller of the soil, became angry with his herdsman brother, Abel. Jealous over God's acceptance of Abel's offering, Cain set forth to mislead, attack, and kill his brother (Genesis 4:2-8).

In judgment, the Lord placed Cain under a curse of ground that "will no longer yield its crops for you." This first-born of the whole human family was assigned to be a restless wanderer on the earth.

Believing that his punishment was more than he could bear, Cain went out from the presence of the Lord and lived in the land of Nod, east of Eden.

And there . . . he built a city (Genesis 4:17).

This, then, becomes the pattern. As soon as the human group arrives at what can be termed civilization, it assumes concrete form as a city. Civilization is expressed by cities. The city becomes the focal point for all human activities: economic, artistic, intellectual, religious, and social, not to mention governmental.

Following the great flood, Noah's sons and their

descendants became nations that spread out over the earth. Those who settled in the plain of Shinar said, "Come, let us build ourselves a city, with a tower that reaches to the heavens, so that we may make a name for ourselves and not be scattered over the face of the whole earth" (Genesis 11:4).

In the search for self-sufficiency, fame, and security, city building begins. And millennia later the same needs drive men to erect cities . . . monuments to Cain, the first to shed innocent blood . . . monuments of restless resentment against divine restraint . . . monuments of a self-centered independence.

FROM THE LAND OF NOD TO BABYLON

Man needs man. But out of this reality grows another: Because of sin's entrance into the world, man cannot get along with man.

As social beings we need community and a life of interdependence. But sin in the human life spawns self-love and self-gratification—acidic forces which eat away at the very mutual love and respect on which communities must exist. We build cities . . . and surrender community! We build our "Babylons" of power, fame, and security . . . and find ourselves powerless, without human dignity, and totally lacking in security. (Visit the city dwellers with their fences and alarm systems, their triple door locks, and concrete vertical villages—where all are strangers.)

Babylon, then, becomes representative of all the cities of men. Each stands as a symbol of man's attempt to regain the power he has lost through sin.

Men still seek their fame and fortune in the city. Towers of steel and stone reach toward the heavens. The city becomes a source of great ideological developments, but all the while crime, ignorance, poverty, and injustice fester in the alleys.

An eminent urbanologist once explained to me that cities are like the human body. As the body has a skeletal system which serves as the scaffold, the framework to support and enclose the rest of the body, the city has its buildings and factories, its stores and houses, its museums and monuments together forming the city's skeletal system. The streets and broad avenues, railroads, waterways, and airports form the city's supply system as surely as arteries and veins form the circulatory system of the body. Supply depots and garbage dumps represent its digestive and excreting capabilities. And telephones, media, and computers constitute the city's nervous system.

But just as death is present in the life of the human body, death haunts the city as well.

Babylon, the great city, stands as a biblical symbol of death. While it is called The Great City and The City of Power, it is also referred to as "the Mother of Prostitutes and of the Abominations of the earth," a home for demons, and a haunt for every evil spirit.

Babylon the Great symbolizes the ultimate of man's power, but it is the power of alienation, it is the power of death.

A TALE OF TWO CITIES

Leave Manila's garbage mound, drive eight short miles, and you will enter the district called "Forbes Park." Broad tree-lined boulevards lead up to its massive church and well-manicured park and polo grounds. The wide avenues are regularly intersected by small roads leading through impressive stone pillars which support strong steel gates. Behind the gates, through the palm and acacia trees, half-hidden by lush tropical foliage, you can catch a glimpse of magnificent mansions. With their broad tile roofs, endless verandas, and intricately-cut stonework, these are the private homes of Manila's society elite. Unlike the residents of nearby Garbage Mountain, these "beautiful people" do not reflect on some future hope of heaven. Why should they, with their own private earthly paradise to enjoy?

The contrast between the garbage-dump slum and the Forbes Park mansions is no greater than the contrast between

Babylon and Jerusalem. Just as scriptural Babylon represents all that is evil and debased, Jerusalem represents the City of God, that shining city upon a hill.

In the Old Testament, Jerusalem was symbolic of the power, wealth, and prestige gained by the chosen people of God. Its Davidic palace and wondrous temple witnessed to the presence, favor, and blessing of Israel's God.

In New Testament times, the ancient city represented both a heritage lost and a hope deferred. The heavy boot of Rome's occupying armies was constant reminder to each Jewish citizen that they were captives in their own land. But Jerusalem, with its temple and towers, its gates and gardens, stood as a constant source of hope. One day . . . one day the kingdom would be regained . . . one day there would be peace, prosperity, and freedom.

In the final book of the New Testament, Jerusalem symbolizes regained hopes, fulfilled dreams, and kingdom glory reborn. John saw "the Holy City, the new Jerusalem, coming down out of heaven . . . prepared as a bride beautifully dressed for her husband" (Revelation 21:2). This New Jerusalem "shone with the glory of God. . . . the Lord God Almighty and the Lamb are its temple. . . . the glory of God gives it light. . . . The glory and honor of the nations will be brought into it" (Revelation 21:11, 22, 23, 26).

CITIES IN CONTRAST

Babylon and Jerusalem . . . the City of Man and the City of God.

Babylon represents all man can achieve in his own strength. Jerusalem demonstrates what God accomplishes in his power.

Babylon, a concentration of evil institutions under the proud banner, "I Did It My Way." Jerusalem, a submission to the power and authority of God under the banner, "His Way—All the Way!"

Babylon, in its quest for human power, breeds *activists* who attempt in their own energy to overthrow evil—thereby creating a vacuum to be filled by another evil more destructive than the first. Jerusalem gives birth to *advocates* who in the authority of God stand with the suffering and oppressed—ever ready to share their pain and to plead their cause.

Babylon is the place of *confrontation,* Jerusalem the spirit of *reason.*

Babylon spawns *revolution* in its attempt to overthrow evil; Jerusalem, through its moral and spiritual resources, creates a *resistance* against "the evil one."

Babylon is a place of endless debate, Jerusalem a place of fervent *prayer.*

Babylon is pervaded by a latent *hostility;* Jerusalem presents itself in a lasting *humility.*

Babylon was created through *human intervention;* Jerusalem is a witness of *divine intervention.*

The Babylons of this world—for all their temporal allure—can produce nothing but *violence, despair,* and *death.* Jerusalem, God's eternal shining city, is always the place of *peace* and *hope* and *life.*

Babylon represents all of the systems, organizations, and power structures man has devised to control, subjugate, and ultimately destroy. Jerusalem is God's Kingdom presence in his people—today in his Church—where he is in control, where his Spirit provides meaning, strength, and fulfillment, and where his good news brings health and hope.

BABYLON—CITY OF MAN

In chapter 6 we considered *personal* evil. But evil can also be *institutional.*

Institutions are more than just groups of human beings organized around some specific idea, task, or goal: they take on a personality, a character, an existence all of their own.

We are reluctant to believe this. It's hard to take that

thought seriously. But to neglect this reality is as serious as neglecting the reality of personal sin and evil.

Look carefully at the building program launched on the plain of Shinar. The issue was more than simply a tower—it was the conception of a new evil!

As a builder, man uses more than mortar to hold the stones of his cities together. Each brick, board, and rod of steel is impregnated with his restless struggle for independence—his ceaseless rebellion against God and God's ways.

City-building continues to this day . . . the hope for life and meaning apart from God's life and meaning. We may call our cities the emerald city, the show city, the rose city, the brilliant or garden or fun city, but all cities—all institutions—built by humankind are manifestations of Babylon. This is their essential nature. They cannot be reformed. The prophet Jeremiah cries out:

> "Flee from Babylon!
>   Run for your lives!
>   Do not be destroyed because of her sins.
> It is time for the Lord's vengeance;
>   he will pay her what she deserves. . . .
> Babylon will suddenly fall and be broken.
>   Wail over her!
> Get balm for her pain;
>   perhaps she can be healed.
>
> "'We would have healed Babylon,
>   but she cannot be healed;
> let us leave her and each go to his own land,
>   for her judgment reaches to the skies'"
>   (Jeremiah 51:6, 8-9).

THE MANY FACES OF BABYLON

Babylon, representative of the accumulated, organized, and controlled powers of humankind, is the product of man's effort and will. The urbanologist's strategic planning, the engineer's broad eye, and the politician's clever mind seek fame and security through their city building, but ultimately bring only slavery and slums, depersonalization and despair.

Cain satisfies his desire for eternity by producing children. He satisfies his desire for security by building a city. In the anonymity of the city he can truly be himself. Here is the place where he can rule and be self-sufficient. But in exchanging God's garden for man's city, he experiences only spiritual and social regression rather than progress. It is so in every attempt at human development which excludes God, his redemptive purposes and power. Each step is a new step in disobedience if it doesn't lead us back to God.

Human arrogance and pride become the chief forces employed to build our cities of refuge and security. In them we concentrate the presence of personal sin and thereby *institutionalize* evil.

Institutionalized evil is a primary obstacle to all schemes for human development. Bureaucratic routine triumphs over human need in the administration of our social welfare and public health programs. Prisons, allegedly built to reform, become a means for banishing and brutalizing certain elements of society the "powers" have found to be unacceptable. All too many government-sponsored public housing schemes have contributed to a form of racial or economic apartheid by imposing racial limitations or by controlling access to credit.

Government reservations formed to preserve and control our Native American population have resulted in cultural and social genocide. Land reform programs continually fall into the greedy hands of a powerful few who use their influence to determine government policy. Private militias, rural and urban terrorists, and state security police enslave the powerless while they purport to protect the weak. The farmer is "developed" in his agricultural resources and techniques, only to see the fruits of his efforts taken from him by marketing forces which can totally control the price he receives for his product. Government-supported social welfare institutions created to alleviate the poverty and suffering of the masses become bastions of personal privilege for the civil-servant class who desire to serve only themselves.

Legislative policies with fine-sounding names promise to "free the people" from this and that, but only further enslave through entangling red tape and unfair catering to special interests. Government institutions which speak widely and grandly about freedom, prosperity, and justice ultimately wield their power in the way they know best: by taxing, regulating, and imprisoning.

The "powers" of this world are legion. They exist, ultimately, in order to dominate and enslave those whom they claim to serve. By denying truth, "managing" and manipulating facts, and covering their actions in a cloak of secrecy, they seek first to deceive—and then to control. Their speech is marked by exaggeration and demagoguery. They defame the weak and demoralize the powerless.

At Babel, the languages were confused. Babylon is the city of Babel. It is here our faculties of comprehension, of sanity, and of conscience are assaulted by untruth. Listen to the voice of Alexander Solzhenitsyn:

> Let us not forget that violence does not exist by itself and cannot do so; it is necessarily interwoven with lies. Violence finds its only refuge in falsehood, falsehood its only support in violence. Any man who has once acclaimed violence as his method must inexorably choose falsehood as his principle.

Any development project, any social concern of human beings which neglects to understand the reality of "principalities and powers" is a deluded effort. Social change empowered by human power alone is doomed to failure. It doesn't matter whether it arises from "the social gospel" or from a deep sense of personal pietism. If it isn't done in the power of Christ and based upon the authority of Scripture, it will fail.

THE RELIGION OF BABYLON

Civil religion may very well be Babylon's most subtle—and dangerous—face. It is the means through which those who possess the power attempt to sanctify their human efforts. Whether it be the emperor worship of ancient Rome or modern Japan, the Islamic jihad of contemporary radical Muslim states, or the amalgamation of Judeo-Christian heritage and national pride and patriotism which marks much of contemporary American religious beliefs and practices, civil religion is a false religion. To interpret the Bible for the convenience of any nation-state is to do radical violence to both the character and content of the biblical message. *All* earthly powers are representative of Babylon. Only the Church, the Kingdom of God, may dare identify itself as Jerusalem. For the state to lust after "the holy nation" status when we speak of the divine destiny of nations is nothing short of idolatry.

Civil religion, writes Jim Wallis, "casts national aspirations and ambitions in religious metaphors, speaks of transcendent moral values, mixes piety with patriotism, invokes God's name when speaking of the national destiny, and generally blurs the distinctions between biblical faith and cultural religion." We must constantly remind ourselves that America is not Jerusalem, that no institution can become the "shining city on the hill." In all our programs of human development, therefore, we guard against resting our confidence in Babylon.

Babylon and all the schemes and plans which rest upon its seemingly secure foundation will fall. Jerusalem and that which is empowered by God's Spirit will stand forever.

Oppression, enslavement, and *death* are the end result of man's city-building. Cain, receiving dominion over all creation, now bends creation to do his will. It is characteristic of man's sinful nature that when faced with a curse, we attempt to fix things rather than repent. Babylon is a symbol of man's attempt to repair the damage . . . an attempt that actually leads to the undoing of all creation.

"Am I my brother's keeper?" (Genesis 4:9). Cain's reply to an inquiring God reflects societal attitudes toward social responsibility. We violate the rights of others by denying that we have any obligation to others. This kind of self-love on an individual level leads to all manner of disorder on a societal level. The resulting chaos becomes the breeding ground for all manner of institutionalized injustice. In Pope John Paul II's most recent visit to North America, he warned that the poor will judge "those who build an imperialistic monopoly of economic and political supremacy at the expense of others. . . . The poor South will judge the rich North. . . . And the poor people and poor nations—poor in different ways, not only lacking in food but also deprived of freedom and other human rights—will judge those people who take these goods away from them, amassing to themselves the monopoly of economic and political supremacy at the expense of others."

Babylon, which promises to become the Gate of the Gods, is inevitably destined to become the Place of Confusion! It is the very gate to hell.

JERUSALEM—CITY OF GOD

"Lovely . . . beautiful . . . majestic and holy . . . a stronghold . . . the joy of the whole earth . . . throne of the Lord . . ."

These are the words used to describe Jerusalem, the City of God. Little wonder that the poet-king spoke of her as "the holy place where the Most High dwells. God is within her, she will not fall" (Psalm 46:4, 5). Although the earthly city of Jerusalem did fall more than once, it is symbolized here as the dwelling place of God among His people.

There have been many "Holy Cities": Thebes for the ancient Egyptians, Lhassa for Tibetans, and Mecca for the world's Muslims, Banaras for Hindus, Rome for Catholics, Geneva for the Reformation and Ecumenical movements, Wheaton for American evangelicals, Richmond for the Southern Baptists, and New York City for the mainline denominations. But Jerusalem, the Holy City of God, illustrious in its history, powerful in its contemporary presence in the Church, and eternal in its future glory, is the dwelling place of God.

THE KINGDOM PRESENCE

Repeatedly the gospels bear witness to the fact that "Jesus went everywhere preaching the good news of the Kingdom of God" (cf. Matthew 4:23; 9:35). In his feeding of the five thousand, he witnesses that the Kingdom is a perfecter of creation; the new order of life lived under Kingdom rule is meant to confront human need in all its dimensions. Jesus rewards those who feed the hungry, clothe the naked, and visit the imprisoned. James says that those who keep the Royal Law are those who care for the needs of brothers and sisters in the faith. "Religion that God our Father accepts as pure and faultless is this: to look after orphans and widows in their distress and to keep oneself from being polluted by the world" (James 1:27).

What a contrast to a civil religion which wraps itself in patriotism, and in the name of God sets forth to manipulate rather than liberate, enslave rather than empower, and enrich itself rather than manifest its generosity to all whom it reaches.

Babylon is a political structure, Jerusalem is a Kingdom presence. Babylon builds its "tower that reaches to the heavens" (Genesis 11:4), but Jerusalem is "built like a city that is closely compacted together" (Psalm 122:3). As such it is a redemptive community actively present in society to initiate and empower spiritual and social change.

KINGDOM PRINCIPLES IN THE CITY

Jerusalem is symbolic of the church, God's redeemed people, expressing themselves as God's active rule on earth. Rather than erecting cities for fame and security, the church is actively creating communities of reconciliation, restoration, and renewal. The Kingdom of God, therefore, is not a place. It is an activity, a happening—it is what God is doing! It is that place where

> the sick are healed,
> the sinner is forgiven,
> the saint is restored.

Stirring within its stimulating fellowship is the creative force for a new community, for the development of human potential, and for the re-creation of all creation.

Dr. William Dyrness writes: "Development is really an extension of the rule of God in the affairs of men . . . whenever genuine human development is taking place it is a reflection of God's own creative and re-creative rule in history." The Kingdom of God is "God's active rule leading to man's salvation and the restoration of the created order."

How Kingdom building differs from City building! The city-builder magnifies the glory of man; the Kingdom-builder emphasizes the dignity and worth of the individual person. He magnifies the glory of God! In the city, men hoard and accumulate. In the Kingdom, the values are placed upon community responsibility and mutual sharing. Babylon attempts to use its power to subjugate and control people. Jerusalem assists people in managing and controlling their environment. Babylon, the city of man, ends in death and despair. Jerusalem, God's Kingdom presence, imparts life and hope.

As the new Jerusalem descended from heaven, flashing with consummate beauty, the apostle John heard a loud voice from the throne:

> "Now the dwelling of God is with men,
>   and he will live with them.
> They will be his people,
>   and God himself will be with them
>   and be their God.
> He will wipe every tear from their eyes.

There will be no more death
  or mourning
  or crying
  or pain,
for the old order of things has passed away"
            (Revelation 21:3,4).

Having ears to hear, the Church responds. But not only with, "Amen, even so come quickly, Lord Jesus" . . . it also responds by allowing itself to become God's Kingdom presence in a broken and shattered world. As we hear and obey, we become that "city on a hill that cannot be hidden" . . . the very light of the world.

"As we have opportunity, let us do good to all people, especially to those who belong to the family of believers" (Galatians 6:10).

Chapter 8

The Church in Mission

*T*he collision occurred at about 10,000 feet as Eastern Airlines flight 597 was making its descent into Miami International.

In a broad, sweeping curve, the plane dipped its wings to the right and sliced through the cloudless sky over the Gold Coast of Florida's eastern shoreline. It was only moments before touchdown, and I was in the process of sketching out the next hour in my mind—and smiling at the prospects.

I'd hurry through customs and immigration—I'm a pro at that—and rush off to my hotel. After the heat, filth, and stifling humidity of Haiti, a long, refreshing shower and a hot fudge sundae would have remarkable restorative powers.

As the plane banked, I looked out over a sparkling array of turquoise jewels—thousands of backyard swimming pools.

That's when the collision occurred. My emotions collided with the conflicting realities of two vastly different worlds.

Superimposed over those clear, cool pools I found myself looking again at a muddy, sewage-infested water hole, the only source of drinking water for an entire Haitian village.

A score of proud church steeples pierced the blue Miami

sky just below me . . . millions of dollars invested in ecclesiastical real estate, many of the facilities used for only a few hours each week . . . and I remembered happy groups of Christians gathered under a large mango tree, singing praises and wishing for a little shelter from the drenching tropical rains.

I caught a last glimpse of beach-front condos, lavish hotels, and a wide bay dotted with a thousand pleasure craft before the 727 screamed onto the tarmac. These were the "good things" of life spoken of in many of those high-spired churches as evidence of God's blessings upon America. I thought about that even as I recalled the filth, disease, and dehumanizing surroundings of the Port-au-Prince slums.

Only yesterday I had worshiped with a few score believers in a tumbledown shack. No spires, no padded pews, no rich-toned pipe organ, no red-carpeted aisles. Just a group of Haitians who called on the name of Jesus. Just a small flicker of hope on a despair-darkened island.

It didn't make sense. I felt angry, frustrated.

"Gold Coasts" and affluent believers . . . luxuriating in their lives of material ease . . . totally oblivious to their Christian brothers and sisters living on "Poverty Coast" just six hundred miles away. "Gold Coasts" rationalized as God's reward to faithful people, while whole communities of believers—practically next door—wonder where tomorrow's food will come from.

People on the plane began crowding into the aisles, gathering up their bags and Haitian "souvenirs." For once I just stayed in my seat, looking out the window at nothing.

Was the God of the "Gold Coast" the same God I encountered in the joyous praises of the "Poverty Coast" believers? How could God handle such disparity? Many of those people in the Miami churches had to rent storage garages to house the overflow of domestic goods! And yet, just minutes away, other sons and daughters of God faced bare shelves, empty stomachs, and withering hopes. How did God put that together?

I gathered up my suitcase, garment bag, and briefcase,

preparing myself for the push and pull of customs. These questions were not going to leave me alone. I needed time—time to work them through. I'd *take* the time. Later, at the hotel . . . but not over a hot-fudge sundae.

THE PRIORITIES OF JESUS

The mid-air emotional ambush I experienced over Miami was part of a long-standing personal struggle. After living in a third world country for a major chunk of my adult life, I frequently find myself wrestling with priority questions. And here's a big one: Has the Western church drifted from a biblical balance in its ministry? Are we really responding to our Lord's priorities?

Think back to the opening days of Christ's ministry. He had returned to Nazareth, the city of his childhood and young adult years. In the course of the Sabbath Day service in the synagogue, the scroll of the prophet was handed to him. Unrolling it, he found the place where it was written:

> "The Spirit of the Lord is on me,
>   because he has anointed me
>   to preach good news to the poor.
> He has sent me to proclaim freedom
>   for the prisoners
>   and recovery of sight for the blind,
> to release the oppressed,
>   to proclaim the year of the Lord's favor"
>   (Luke 4:18,19).

Jesus read the passage, rolled up the scroll, handed it to the worship leader, and returned to his seat. Every eye was fastened on him. He met their gaze, and with simple dignity said, "Today this scripture is fulfilled in your hearing."

Jesus made his agenda clear—right from that beginning place of public ministry. He first proclaimed his Lordship, his right to speak. "The Spirit of the Lord is on me," he said. "He has anointed me."

This is always the starting point for Christian ministry: to reveal and proclaim that Jesus Christ is Lord. In doing so we acknowledge his ownership over our personal lives and over the Church, his body.

Following the proclamation of his Lordship, Jesus proceeded to announce the good news. Matthew's gospel says he went "throughout Galilee . . . preaching the good news" (4:23; 9:35). This "good news" and the word *gospel* are synonymous. God's news in Jesus Christ is the ultimate good news. It is good news because:

It is proclaimed with special concern and meaning for the poor. The Greek word used here is *ptochois*, a New Testament term that speaks of a person who is bowed down, one who occupies an inferior position in society, an outcast. This is a person without means of livelihood, who must beg in order to survive. The poor were Jesus' first priority in ministry.

It is a message which proclaims freedom for the prisoners and healing for the physically disabled. Remember the context for the passage Christ read to the congregation: the prophet Isaiah first spoke these words to a nation of people who "grieve in Zion." Don't spiritualize away the importance of these words to those who were victims of oppression and injustice on the one hand, and troubled by great physical needs on the other. The gospel is "good news" precisely because it has a message of hope and healing, of deliverance.

It is a message which calls us "to release the oppressed." Liberating people involves encounters with "the powers." And Jesus gave to his disciples power and authority, power to drive out evil spirits, power to liberate humankind from demons and human oppression, and power to challenge authorities by the authority of the Word of God and the presence of the Holy Spirit.

THE TWO LEGS OF THE GOSPEL

A few years ago I was conversing on some of these issues with a well-known leader of the American evangelical movement. We had been talking about the important Christian ministry of social responsibility.

I commented, "There are two legs to the gospel—evangelism and social action. If we don't walk or run on both legs, we have a lopsided gospel."

My friend did not agree with my statement. To elevate Christian social action to a place of importance equal with evangelism was to "diminish the gospel," he said.

I disagree with this sort of dualistic thinking, and felt reinforced in my beliefs by the statement released by the Consultation on the Relationship between Evangelism and Social Responsibility:

"Evangelism and Social Responsibility are inseparable fruits of the gospel and basic to the mission of the church. . . . Evangelism and social action belong to each other, like the two blades of a scissors or the two wings of a bird."

The report continued by stating that "social action should be the *consequence* of evangelism, it can be a *bridge* to evangelism, and social action must always be the *partner* of evangelism. . . . Seldom if ever should we have to choose between satisfying physical hunger and spiritual hunger, or between healing bodies and saving souls, since an authentic love for our neighbor will lead us to serve him or her as a whole person."

THE FIFTH SPIRITUAL LAW

The well-known *Four Spiritual Laws* tract begins: "God loves you and has a wonderful plan for your life." Perhaps a fifth spiritual law needs to be added: "God loves you and has a wonderful plan for *their* lives." Salvation and the blessings of the new life were never intended to be focused alone on the one receiving God's mercy and favor. That old cliché is right: We are saved to serve. Not just saved to enjoy . . . not just saved to talk about it . . . but we are saved to do something with the resources and benefits we have received.

James makes this responsibility plain in his letter reminding us that "every good and perfect gift is from above" (1:17).

He then makes clear that the responsibility of the gifted is to "look after orphans and widows in their distress" (1:27). The test of our Christian faith is our willingness to help those in need.

"What good is it, my brothers, if a man claims to have faith but has no deeds? Can such faith save him? Suppose a brother or sister is without clothes and daily food. If one of you says to him, 'Go, I wish you well; keep warm and well fed,' but does nothing about his physical needs, what good is it? In the same way, faith by itself, if it is not accompanied by action, is dead" (James 2:14-17).

To those who would argue that they are gifted in faith but have not received the gift of helps, he sets forth three important principles:

1. The faithless can believe in God, but the faith of the righteous is demonstrated in what is done for others (2:18,19).

2. Abraham's faith and actions working together demonstrated that his faith was made complete by what he did (2:21-23).

3. Just as the body without the spirit is dead, so faith without deeds of kindness is also dead (2:26).

A gospel of works? No, it is a gospel of fruit!

The central message of the apostle John's first epistle is a message of *love*. "This is the message you heard from the beginning: We should love one another" (1 John 3:11). And how does that love manifest itself?

If anyone has material possessions and sees his brother in need but has no pity on him, how can the love of God be in him? (1 John 3:17).

In fact, John makes a case for the assurance of a believer's salvation measured by how that professed believer responds to brothers and sisters in need! The ministries of social concern are hardly set forth as sideline distractions; they are central to what we believe.

A MODEL FOR SERVICE

I was discussing the place and importance of the church with a young university student who, for various reasons he felt were legitimate, was quite disenchanted with the churches he had been personally involved with.

"The problem with the church," he said, "is that they have all the answers. They just don't know what questions people are asking!"

How irrelevant and removed much of the message and ministry of the church has become in a world where millions go to bed hungry each night . . . in a world where children die needlessly from childhood diseases for want of simple and inexpensive immunization . . . in a world where we publish voluminous literature on Christian home life when so many have no homes!

Remember the parable of the good Samaritan (Luke 10:25-37)? A sincere young teacher of the law had come to Jesus with a fundamental question: How can one inherit eternal life? Love God and love your neighbor, Jesus replied. In the argumentative fashion of a good lawyer, the inquirer asked, "And who is my neighbor?"

It was in answer to this question that Jesus gave us that timeless—and often trivialized—parable.

The church today would do well to examine this story and from it develop some important principles for ministry. We dare not forget that the very ones who missed the opportunity of ministry in our Lord's story were two very "religious" men . . . a priest and a Levite. So busy were they in the performance of their religious routine that they had no time for even a cursory examination of the stricken man. No time to discover if he was even alive or dead! But a Samaritan, one who from both a religious and cultural viewpoint would be expected to have little or no contact with a Jew, stopped immediately to help the poor fellow. He ministered to the wounded man's needs, took him where he could receive help, and made a commitment of his

personal resources for the man's use until he was completely recovered.

There are three important principles of ministry here.

1. The help offered was *practical*. "He went to him and
bandaged his wounds, pouring on oil and wine" (Luke 10:34).
No inquiry as to the man's religious beliefs or preferences. The
Samaritan was not "sophisticated" enough in his religious beliefs to argue the priority of evangelism over social action. No
proffered gospel tract with an attempt to convert. Just a simple,
straightforward, practical response to an evident human need.

Dietrich Bonhoeffer, the German churchman who was
later to lose his life at the hands of the Nazis, wrote from his
prison cell: "It is not enough that the church simply proclaim to
the world, she must actually get down into the dirt and grime of
history and participate in the task of remaking the world into
God's kingdom."

That kind of discipleship is costly, but its practicality will
authenticate the "good news" to the poor.

2. The help given reflected a personal *generous* spirit. He
placed the man on the back of his donkey, thereby making it
necessary to shoulder burdens that the pack animal had been
carrying for him. He took the hurting stranger to the local Holiday Inn, and there personally remained to care for him.

It does cost—both the individual and the church—to become involved in helping those in need. It costs us the incon-
venience of disrupted plans, the diversion of resources which
were to be spent on our own needs and wants, and the commitment of time and personal involvement. All these are reflective
of a generous spirit.

3. Finally, the assistance given by the Samaritan was
thorough. Not just a quick "band-aid" response by the side of
the road . . . not a short overnight in the inn . . . this man provided for the wounded traveler until he could resume care for
himself. He gave him cash and then left his *Israeli Express* card
with the innkeeper with instructions to charge everything
needed against his account. There was no paternalism here that

demanded complete and final control over the cash until the desired results were achieved. The Samaritan was willing to trust for positive results to come from his caring act.

The poor of our world need not so much a handout as they need a helping hand. We need to understand their problems and then work with the individuals affected by the problems to help them find a solution. That involves a commitment thorough enough to produce results.

"Give a man a fish," the saying goes, "and you feed him for a day. But teach a man to fish and you feed him for a lifetime."

PENTECOST IS PRACTICAL!

Just as had been promised, the disciples were filled and empowered by the Holy Spirit in that upper room on the day of Pentecost. Immediate results were evident from that infusion of life and power. A timid, confused, leaderless band of disciples was transformed into a band of leaders, bold in their witness. Peter, who days before could not summon up enough courage to answer the questions of a simple Galilean girl, now openly declared to all Jerusalem that the one they crucified was both Lord and Christ!

Many citizens of Jerusalem believed and together formed the First Church of Jerusalem, a church which rapidly discovered her mission. They became eager students of the apostles' teaching. In a warm spirit of love and fellowship, they met together for prayer and communion. Signs, wonders, and miracles accompanied the ministry of the apostles.

And take careful note: These earliest followers of Jesus expressed their new faith by a common concern for the physical— as well as the spiritual—needs of their new community. "All the believers were together and had everything in common. Selling their possessions and goods, they gave to anyone as he had need" (Acts 2:44, 45).

No wonder the Lord added daily to their number! When

the "good news" takes on flesh and blood, people notice.

The very first New Testament church organization grew out of the church's desire to be effective as well as fair in their ministry to the needy. A dispute had arisen between the widows rooted in the Grecian-Jewish community and those who were part of the Aramaic-speaking community. Someone tossed in a charge of "favoritism."

Remember, the church was already busy with discharging their responsibilities of care for the poor among them. It wasn't a question of concern or generosity; there seemed to be no lack of resources to meet the needs of these poor widows. The problem was rather one of a *just distribution system,* because some received more than they needed, while others went without.

The world really hasn't changed all that much in 2,000 years. Many of our poverty problems today are rooted in this same scenario. A billion of our world are hungry—right this moment—and it is not because there are insufficient food supplies for the world's people. The reason men, women, boys, and girls are going without a single meal today is that unjust structures and unfair accumulations of wealth and power lend themselves to top-sided distribution of the resources. Mahatma Gandhi was correct in saying, "This world has enough resources for every man's need, but not enough for every man's greed."

How then can the church become "good news" to this kind of world? We need to rethink our mission. We need to root out all spirit of competition between the various agendas of that mission. And we need to regain balance both in our priorities and in the way we use our resources.

We are called to be global Christians, to have a "whole-world" perspective on ministry. In commissioning his disciples, the risen Lord gave his followers an international, cross-cultural challenge. "Go to *all* the world! Preach the gospel to *every* creature! Disciple *all* nations!"

The apostle Peter wasn't ready for that kind of wide-reaching vision—at first. In his mind, the gospel obviously belonged to the Jews alone. Then came a roof-top vision and the

Lord's clear, cross-cultural directive: The gospel is for Jew and Gentile alike.

In response to a heavenly vision of his own, Paul first took the gospel to the Middle East and then went on to Europe. In those first centuries of Christianity, the good news was carried to all the known world.

There is no room for provincialism or elitism. No group of people must be favored over another in having free access to the good news.

The Church is always God's counter-culture to express to the watching world what life is like when Christ is Lord. The work of the Church in missions is one of demonstrating—demonstrating Christ's love in word and deed. A hurting world is not really concerned all that much about our beliefs. They want to feel our compassionate love. There's an important principle of communication here: *If the behavior of the messenger does not match the message, real communication does not take place.* I remember the words of a little chorus I learned in Vacation Bible School many years ago: "What you are/speaks so loud/that I cannot hear what you say . . . !"

If, however, the Church turns a blind eye and withholds a helping hand from the suffering, oppression, alienation, and loneliness of people, then we should not be surprised when the non-Christian turns a deaf ear to our message of eternal salvation. Only as redeemed men and women *demonstrate* the gospel—only then will it be seen as "good news" by those who are aliens from God's kingdom.

MEANWHILE, BACK IN MIAMI . . .

The suitcase was emptied, the garment bag hung up in the hotel room closet. Exhausted, I threw myself face downward across the bed. The pictures in my mind were more vivid than anything I could have seen from my window.

I saw the narrow, crowded valley in southwest Haiti where World Concern had been working in partnership with a North

American mission agency and the churches of Mission Evangelique Baptiste Sud Haiti. We were trying to help the 12,000 valley residents achieve a little more control over their lives. Hunger and disease permeated the valley like voodoo drums at twilight. Until recently, even the simplest forms of medical care were non-existent. The people were as impoverished as any I had seen anywhere in the world.

I remembered visiting the schoolhouse where children not only learned, but were fed. Most of these children arrived at school having had no breakfast. And the school could provide but one meal—at midday.

"Why don't you call your students to the front of the classroom to recite?" I asked the teacher. "Why don't you use the blackboard? Where are the books?"

I felt ashamed—and sickened—as she explained to me that by midmorning some of the children were too weak from hunger to expend energy on unnecessary movement. Some had not eaten since yesterday's noonday meal! There was little enough money for food; to spend for chalk and other teaching aids had to be second priority. And parents who could scarcely provide the simple clothing their children needed to attend school could hardly afford the extravagance of books.

Lying there on that hotel bed, I thought it seemed a bit unreal that only the day before I had been feted with a simple but abundant meal in the house of the local pastor and his family. The most generous people in the world are its poor! Pastor Enil and his family knew hunger as an experience, not just as a statistic. The diseases and death brought by hunger had touched their home, their own precious children.

Their generosity, though deeply appreciated, had made me feel uncomfortable, if not a bit ashamed.

I wanted to sleep, but couldn't. I kept thinking about that schoolroom full of hungry kids . . . and their parents, home trying to scratch out a living on the infertile rocky hillsides . . . and dear Pastor Enil.

I was troubled. Restless. Totally drained. One could find

no more dedicated servants of Christ than the pastor and his loving, gracious wife. His family life reflected the best in Christian virtue. His ministry among the poor of the valley was selfless and sensitive. The unresolved question of his poverty and my affluence went around and around in my head—and in my gut.

I had to find some answers, or at the very least find solace for my troubled spirit. My Bible always seemed to fall open to the Psalms in times like those. I craved the balm of those ancient songs—literally thirsted for the familiar strains of trust and hope and confidence.

I leafed quickly to one of my favorite chapters. Here I would surely find the comfort I needed.

But the comfort wasn't there. Instead, a verse leaped out at me from the well-worn page with the force of a blow to the jaw. The words I saw startled me at first—and then made me angry. My anger was at God, for this was his Word, and I couldn't find its truth. I read: "For as long as I have lived, I have never seen the righteous hungry, or their children begging bread" (Psalm 37:25).

Untrue! Hunger is no respecter of persons! I have seen as many Christians hungry as non-Christians. Doubt swept over me like a cold wave. How could the psalmist say such a thing? It was a lie. All my life I had believed every word of Scripture. But this . . .

Fortunately, as I meditated and reasoned my anger diminished into thoughtfulness. What could this verse of Scripture mean? I began to remember God's gracious concern for the poor evidenced throughout human history:

> a perfect garden at the beginning of history;
> an ark of safety and provision for Noah and his
>   family;
> abundance promised and provided for Abraham;
> Joseph's friendship with Pharaoh which provided
>   food in a time of famine;
> manna in the desert and fresh water for the thirsty
>   from the rock.

And I thought of the various laws God had given his people to protect the rights and to provide for the needs of the poor:

> cancellation of debt and return of property in the year of Jubilee;
> harvest laws which always left ungleaned grain in the field for the widow and orphan, the wayfarer and stranger;
> tithes of grain to be used for the poor;
> temple offerings to provide for those who had not received their needed share of basic resources for living.

I remembered the prophets' condemnation of those who exploit the poor, and their call to the people of God to show justice and mercy to the needy.

I remembered Jesus feeding the hungry, healing the broken-hearted, restoring sight to the blind, freeing the captive.

I remembered the early church's concern for their poor, evidenced first in the distribution of goods, then later by the offerings of the saints collected by the apostle Paul for the hungry in Jerusalem.

And then at last I began to understand these words of the psalmist. He was speaking here of intention, God's intention for the needy and their children. He was speaking here of potential, what *can* be when God's people live according to God's plan. He was speaking here of stewardship and responsibility.

God has no hands but our hands. God's resources to feed the hungry, clothe the naked, and shelter the homeless are those resources he has placed in our hands.

The Church's mission, then, is to *be* the people of God witnessing to his active presence in history. And this witness will always make the greatest impact when touching lives, healing hurts, delivering people from oppression, and announcing the coming of the Kingdom of God.

And I understood! Life lived God's way will never find the righteous hungry or their children begging bread.

Part 3

"Give, and it will be given to you. A good measure, pressed down, shaken together and running over. . . . For with the measure you use, it will be measured to you" (Luke 6:38).

"Our desire is not that others might be relieved while you are hard pressed, but that there might be equality . . . your plenty will supply what they need . . . their plenty will supply what you need" **(2 Corinthians 8:13, 14).**

Chapter 9

Faithful Stewards

"**I**gziabiher yistilign!" I had just presented a check to my Ethiopian businessman friend. The money was to be used to help purchase supplies for the children's feeding program in one of the poorer sections of Addis Ababa.

The words in the local language were spoken by a young boy I had met earlier that morning. The directors of the program had found him at a local bus station. Gaunt-faced and with the too-slender frame of a body denied adequate nutrition, he had been brought, dirty and lonely, to the center. His only clothes were the dirty rags clinging to his unwashed skin.

But now a smile crossed his face as he said to me, "Igziabiher yistilign!" I asked my host the meaning of those words.

"May the Lord return it to you," he said. It was a courteous, local custom to give this greeting when one had done a favor, or performed a caring service. I had been the one trying to bring a blessing to others, yet time after time I received this grateful blessing in return.

This same spirit of thankfulness and generosity marked each contact I had with the little people of HOPE centers and schools in Ethiopia.

I remembered the little girl, horribly scarred, sitting at a table sorting peanuts. Her hands were little more than clubs. Her face . . . it made me want to turn away, half out of shock, half from embarrassment.

They told me her story. Her little brother had fallen into the kitchen fire. The eight-year-old sister had plunged fearlessly into the flames, and with clothes ablaze, flesh incinerating, saved the boy's life. But now this brave sister's body was deformed for life. At first, she could not close her eyes. The fire had burned away her eyelids. Large patches of flesh had been charred. Through the heavy scars I could see that before the surgeries the fire had left only a half-face.

HOPE took her in. Though there were remaining surgeries, she now had a chance to live, to be accepted, to learn a trade and become self sufficient.

And she is saying to *me* . . . "Igziabiher yistilign!"

LIFE'S EXCHANGE SYSTEM

What an incredible exchange system life creates! One person's sorrows and sufferings become another person's opportunity to experience joy and fullness. And that joy and fullness of the giving person spills over into the life of the suffering person. That's what our Lord's promise implies.

Give and you will receive.

Share and it will be returned to you.

Creating opportunities for giving only creates new avenues of receiving! Keep what you have by giving it away. Save through losing. What a phenomenal rewards system for all those who would take the risk to share.

In the past ten years I have come face to face with the poor and deprived in more than eighty countries. As a relief and development professional, I have been in the business of doing for others. Confronting such a magnitude of human suffering, I am often asked how I can emotionally bear up. The one asking the question has usually never fully experienced the returns we receive when we give our lives away.

The begging leper in a smelly, darkened pedestrian underpass in Madras places his hands together in a prayer-like fashion. His spoken "Namiste!" thanking me for my help more than rewards me for what is given up and creates a warm glow on the brutalized face of suffering.

The heartfelt gratitude of arriving refugees crawling from the bowels of the putrid little boat is more than enough to compensate our refugee camp workers for the long hours, spartan diets, and noisy, crowded living quarters.

Then there was the village lady in the remote northeastern region of Bangladesh. What could be more humbling—and rewarding—than to hear her say, "If you had not come, my children all would have died." Malnutrition, dysentery, and tuberculosis had killed her older children. With inoculations, adequate food and nutrition, sanitation and clean drinking water, hope for a future for her children was now rekindled.

And what did that Laotian farmer say to me? "I thought no Americans cared." The farmer had lost both legs, one just above the ankle and the other below the knee. A discarded American bomb . . . a terrible explosion while he plowed his field . . . had changed his life forever. The new prosthetic devices we had just fitted to his shattered legs were crude and awkward by some standards, but the farmer's heart overflowed with gratitude. He could follow the plow again!

Poor food, hot hotel rooms, and missed airport connections were forgotten in a moment. I had given—and the Lord had returned it all to me once again!

SIX MEALS ON THE SIDEWALK

This beautiful transaction of giving and receiving is a delightful aspect of biblical stewardship. But where does stewardship begin? It may begin with a simple awareness of what we already have.

Here is a case in point:

The other morning I found my breakfast on the sidewalk of a downtown Seattle street. And my lunch. And my dinner.

And enough food for all three meals tomorrow, too.

Downtown for an early meeting, I had passed the entrance to one of the city's exclusive private clubs. There on the sidewalk was rice . . . lots of it. Obviously it had been thrown to celebrate some happy couple's marriage. But for me it memorialized another couple's hunger.

Stooping over, I scraped up the uncooked grains of rice from the cold cement. I was able to retrieve just under nine ounces. I remembered that this was more rice than many refugees I had served would receive for a day's ration. Though only half the minimum requirement, it represented triple the food that millions of Africans would have available during that continent's frequent famines.

Six meals. Two days of breakfast, lunch, and dinner, thrown out into the streets. Seeing it there reminded me of my blessings . . . but also of another man's hunger. Confronting that parable on the sidewalk, I asked my Lord for a heart with new awareness: to become aware of my blessings . . . aware of the greatness of my resources . . . aware of all the opportunities I have to live with just a little less so others might just live.

"Man over the House"

In biblical language the word *stewardship* is best understood as "the man over the house."

It is a word of privilege, but also of responsibility. It implies trust, but reminds one of obligation.

Stewardship is never assumed. It is always given by the one who owns the resources. God has made us stewards of creation; we are to tend and care for it. We are stewards of our material resources; we are accountable to use them wisely and generously. We are stewards of the mysteries of God; all he has given us in Christ is to be shared with others while enjoyed by ourselves.

In a world where so many suffer need while a few squander excess, we need a fresh understanding of stewardship.

House majority leader Jim Wright of Texas told an overflow audience at a National Press Club luncheon: "If we had begun spending one million dollars a day from the birth of Christianity, we still would not have spent quite half the 1.6 trillion which our president would earmark for military spending in five years. If political leadership has a role to play, surely it is ours in Congress and in America to rearrange this grotesque misuse of our God-given treasure."

A generation ago, then-President Dwight D. Eisenhower, who himself served as a five-star general in World War II, spoke as "one who has witnessed the horror and the lingering sadness of war—as one who knows that another war could utterly destroy this civilization which has been so slowly and painfully built over thousands of years."

He went on to observe that "every gun that is made, every warship launched, every rocket fired, signifies in a final sense a theft from those who hunger and are not fed, those who are cold and are not clothed. This world in arms is not spending money alone—it is spending the sweat of its laborers, the genius of its scientists, the houses of its children."

These are not the words of some naive "peacenik," but rather the prophetic soundings of a statesman with a clear view of humankind's stewardship of resources.

In one year of social spending, President Lyndon Johnson, remembered for a "butter and guns" national economic policy, even at the height of his "Great Society" programs spent an amount equal to only *three weeks* of military spending in Vietnam. Such profligate waste must be judged by sound stewardship principles.

Today most of the world's peoples are poor. In Africa alone, more than 100 million face starvation. Two-thirds of the world's deaths are caused by hunger or problems related to hunger. Because of human selfishness and humankind's unwillingness to assume its responsibility of stewardship—*man over the house*—the world has become filled with all kinds of injustice and oppression. The fourth-century Patriarch of Constantinople, John Chrysostom, said of his contemporaries:

You eat to excess; Christ eats not even what he needs. You eat a variety of cakes; he eats not even a piece of dried bread. You drink fine Thracian wine; but on him you have not bestowed so much as a cup of cold water. You lie on a soft and embroidered bed; but he is perishing in the cold. . . . You live on things that properly belong to him. Why, were you the guardian of a child and, having taken control of his estate, you neglected him in his extreme need, you would have ten thousand answers and you would suffer the punishment set by law. At the moment, you have taken possession of the resources that belong to Christ and you consume them aimlessly. Don't you realize that you are going to be held accountable?

David Moberg, a prominent contemporary sociologist, reminds us that "The Great Reversal goes on." Where once evangelism and social concern were separated, causing a great theological chasm, today many Americans, many Christians among them, live with a far greater chasm: the disparity in life styles between us and the rest of the world. Instead of working to make the impoverished of our world better off, all too many of us get caught up in the spirit of that recent political slogan, *Are we better off than we were four years ago?* Far too many twentieth-century evangelicals identify with the mainstream values of wealth and power rather than concerning themselves with the needs of the poor.

Jim Wallis writes: "The church in the United States is rich. Christians happily participate in our national lifestyle, which is consuming forty percent of the earth's resources for a mere six percent of the world's people. That fact is a sin against Christ. Resources are dwindling. The poor are becoming hungrier while the appetites of the rich show little sign of subsiding. . . . When we see a church that has fallen into accumulation and affluence, a church that is being consumed by its own consumption, we are witnessing a church that has fallen into idolatry."

Small wonder that the rich man's face fell when Jesus, in response to the man's question about eternal life, said: "One thing you lack. . . . Go, sell everything you have and give to the poor, and you will have treasure in heaven. Then come, follow me" (Mark 10:21).

Danger! Beware! The Scriptures abound with warnings about the adverse effect riches can have upon the Christian life.

STRANGLING ON ABUNDANCE

In Jesus' parable of the sower, he warns that "the deceitfulness of wealth" and "the desires for other things" can *choke* all fruitfulness from the life of a believer (Matthew 13:22, Mark 4:19). Jobs and activities, houses and cars, swimming pools and hot tubs, water skies and snowmobiles, stock markets and investment portfolios—these are the experiences and values of life that can, if not kept properly in balance, actually strangle a Christian's spiritual life and maturity.

WEIGHED DOWN BY ABUNDANCE

Jesus said to his disciples, "Do not worry about your life, what you will eat; or about your body, what you will wear. Life is more than food, and the body more than clothes" (Luke 12:22, 23). He invites them to learn from the birds, observe the clothing of the lily, recognize the uncertainty of a single hour of life. Why then do we worry? Living irresponsibly in a world of need colors our yesterdays with guilt and preordains our tomorrows for worry.

> *What if my house burns down?*
> *How can I protect my investment?*
> *What if the stock market falls?*
> *Could the burglar alarm fail?*
> *Should I have parked my "Z" in a far corner of the*
>   *lot?*

These are the worries that bring collapse to far too many. Jesus had a great defense against worry over material possessions. "Do not be afraid, little flock, for your Father has been pleased to give you the kingdom. Sell your possessions and give to the poor. Provide purses for yourselves that will not wear out, a treasure in heaven that will not be exhausted, where no thief comes near and no moth destroys" (Luke 12:32, 33).

What a liberating view of possessions! To truly own instead of being possessed! Free to surrender, rather than enslaved by the need to preserve.

One of my friends was being shown through a Calcutta orphanage. Mother Teresa was showing Barry babies that had been rescued from garbage cans—little boys and girls whose home heretofore had been beside the city dump.

Impressed with both the needs and the opportunity, Barry asked her what he could do to help these poor children. Pointing to his shirt, Mother Teresa said, "Next time when you go out to buy this for fifteen dollars, I want you to give fifteen dollars to the poor also. Give an amount equal to what you are using for yourself!"

What a lesson in sharing! What a cure for worry!

BLINDED BY ABUNDANCE

Someone has well said, "Our pocketbooks have more to do with heaven and hell than our hymnbooks." Jesus told the story of the rich man who had everything, and a beggar who had nothing. The rich man, blinded by his abundance, neither saw his need for righteousness nor prepared himself for eternity. Lazarus, who had received only bad things, "crumbs from the rich man's table," had prepared well for his future. And their roles in the future life were completely reversed! (Luke 16:19-31) The wealthy man's abundance bought him an eternal curse.

The blessings and woes recorded in Luke chapter 6 give an even clearer understanding of our Lord's teachings on wealth, poverty, and responsibility. What a contrast to our understanding!

Blessed Are:	Woe To:
You poor	You that are rich
You that hunger now	You that are full now
You that weep now	You that laugh now
You when men hate you	You when all men speak well of you (Luke 6:17-26).

The apostle Paul warns against covetousness. "[No] greedy person . . . has any inheritance in the kingdom of Christ and of God" (Ephesians 5:5). He instructs young Timothy, "Godliness with contentment is great gain. . . . if we have food and clothing, we will be content with that. People who want to get rich fall into temptation and a trap and into many foolish and harmful desires that plunge men into ruin and destruction. For the love of money is a root of all kinds of evil" (1 Timothy 6:6-10).

Confucius had more than his usual wisdom when a king once asked his advice on what to do about the large number of thieves stealing his treasures.

Confucius answered, "If you, sir, were not covetous, although you should reward them to do it, they would not steal." What an enormous burden is on those favored by the rules!

CHAINED BY ABUNDANCE

How tragic that so many confuse the issue of a responsible use of wealth by rationalizing the disparities between rich and poor.

"Serve the King and prosper!" is the good—and damnably false—news of a gospel of affluence.

"We'll always have the poor with us—Jesus said so!" is the cop-out on responsibility for some.

"I'm a faithful tither!" others insist, without understanding that to whom much is given, much is required.

Ron Sider's ideas on the "graduated tithe," set forth in *Rich Christians in an Age of Hunger,* would free up enormous resources for the task of world evangelization, as well as for caring ministries which would help heal the hurts, right the wrongs, and bring help and hope to the poor of our world.

"Storehouse tithing," which recently resulted in a thirty-two million dollar building complex—complete with eight bowling alleys, swimming pools, gymnasiums, and health clubs—for a Baptist church in Texas, is an offense to the gospel of Jesus Christ. It is totally out of place in a world of such incredible need.

"One thing remains clear," writes Orlando Costas, "it takes more than the deliberations of conferences, congresses, councils and commissions, more than the refined language of theological statements, for the gospel to penetrate the many life situations of man and liberate him from the power of sin. . . . It takes the outpouring of the Spirit of God. . . . It takes the absolute commitment of the church to the Gospel. . . . It takes the humiliation of the church, *her voluntary impoverishment* for the sake of Christ and the world for whom he died."

American Christians must be delivered from the tragic distortions of reality which makes us think "we are just getting by." The facts reveal that we live better than ninety percent of the world's inhabitants. It may be true that you are "barely keeping up with the bills," but the problem is probably not one of too many expenses but rather of too great expectations. All too many of us are buried up to our necks in bills. Our futures are mortgaged! The pressures that result from these unmet financial obligations place enormous strains on our personal and family lives, compromising our ability to serve others for Jesus' sake. The consumer system enslaves us rather than frees us.

Cyprian, the third-century bishop of Carthage, wrote an amazingly up-to-date description of the affluent:

> Their property held them in chains . . . chains which shackled their courage and choked their faith and hampered their judgment and throttled their souls. . . . If they stored up their treasure in heaven,

they would not now have an enemy and a thief within their household. . . . They think of themselves as owners, whereas it is they rather who are owned: enslaved as they are to their own property, they are not the masters of their money but its slaves.

How we need to hear the voice of the New Testament as it calls us to a life of responsible stewardship of our resources.

"Do not store up for yourselves treasures on earth. . . . But store up for yourselves treasures in heaven . . . For where your treasure is, there your heart will be also. . . . No one can serve two masters. . . . You cannot serve both God and Money" (Matthew 6:19-21,24).

"Then he said to them, 'Watch out! Be on your guard against all kinds of greed; a man's life does not consist in the abundance of his possessions' " (Luke 12:15).

"This is how we know what love is: Jesus Christ laid down his life for us. And we ought to lay down our lives for our brothers. If anyone has material possessions and sees his brother in need but has no pity on him, how can the love of God be in him? Dear children, let us not love with words or tongue but with actions and in truth" (1 John 3:16-18).

We are called to a life of selfless service, to a radical stewardship which places all we possess at the disposal of the one we call Lord.

FAITHFUL STEWARDS

Who, then, is this person that the Bible calls a "faithful steward"?

A faithful steward is one freed from the tyranny of possessions, the anxiety of ownership, and the paralyzing fear of loss.

It would be simplistic to believe that we can exist in this life without possessing any of this world's goods. The ragged beggar on the streets of any third-world city pushes his handmade cart before him, filled with the discarded possessions of more fortunate city dwellers: a pile of rags, a broken wheel, half of a doll, and a few cracked and chipped dishes. A broken, half-rotted window frame, about ready to topple off the pile, represents his dream for the house he'll never own. Pitiful as they may seem to us, these are his *possessions,* and he will defend them with his life.

What liberty, however, when we are forced from the anxiety of ownership. It liberates us from our worries and releases us to spend and be spent for others. We never really know how important our possessions are until they have been taken from us, or until we willingly take the inevitable risk to surrender them—all of them—to God.

A faithful steward is one who responds because others have needs, not just because he can afford to. A romantic Hollywood movie of a number of years ago made famous a silly and senseless definition of love. "Love," gushed Ryan O'Neal, "means you never have to say you're sorry." I can't even imagine what is meant by such trite words. A faithful steward will give you a different definition: *love is acting spontaneously and sacrificially to meet needs.*

This kind of love is *unselfish:* it gives without regard for the cost.

This quality of love is *unconditional:* it places no obligations on the one who receives the benefits.

This is a love that is *unending:* it places no limits upon its extent. It has that same quality of thoroughness we noted in an earlier chapter in the kindness of the Good Samaritan.

A faithful steward recognizes the relationship between spiritual renewal and compassionate economics. Acts 2:42-47 and Acts 4:32-35 reveal a direct relationship between personal piety and community sharing. Those who were filled with the Holy Spirit, ignited by heavenly fire, and emboldened by Pentecostal power were the same believers who, "selling their possessions and goods . . . gave to anyone as he had need" (Acts 2:45). Those who were "filled with the Holy Spirit and spoke the word of God boldly. . . . [who] were one in heart and mind" were the same believers who claimed no personal possession as their own, "but they shared everything that they had" (Acts 4:31, 32). Is it, then, any great wonder that the apostles' witness to the resurrection of the Lord Jesus carried with it such power, such authenticity?

Nothing lends as much credibility to a gospel of love as eliminating the needs of the needy among us by the spontaneous sharing of the people of God.

A faithful steward is one who excels in the grace of giving. The apostle Paul recognized the generosity of the Macedonian believers who extended assistance to those suffering in Jerusalem. Out of the most severe trial, their overflowing joy and their extreme poverty welled up in rich generosity.

Overflowing joy. Extreme poverty. Rich generosity. To those of us so accustomed to being possessed by our possessions, these are difficult words to understand. The words seem to be in disharmony. How in the world can overflowing joy, extreme poverty, and rich generosity fit together?

That question takes me back to a memorable Sunday dinner.

Following a three-hour-long morning service, I was invited to the pastor's home for dinner, certainly not in itself an unusual event to one as accustomed to Sunday fried-chicken fare as I was. For three decades as an itinerant pastor, traveling evangelist, and globe-wandering missionary, I had been the beneficiary of more fried chicken, dry, thinly-sliced ham, and slippery green peas than many of you.

But there was a difference in this invitation. A crowded wood house with thatch roof and cleanly-swept dirt floor was home to this pastor and his family in southwest Haiti. I was the honored guest, and was embarrassed when they insisted I occupy the only chair in the sparsely-furnished room. Freshly-laundered curtains, a faded plastic rose placed in a clay pot, and a few magazine covers and calendar pictures tacked to the grim, unpainted wall could not hide the absolute poverty of this home.

While I sat and waited during the meal preparation, I

mused about this dear family, so poor in this world's goods, so dedicated to living a life of selfless service before the people in their poverty-filled village. I knew that the pastor and his family could scarcely survive on their small stipend and the few fruits and vegetables donated by dedicated but impoverished parishioners. I knew that this godly couple had already buried several of their children, all dying from malnutrition or easily-preventable childhood diseases. I knew their remaining children walked barefoot to school, studied in schoolrooms without books, and sacrificed the noon meal each day to pay for the inadequate village education.

The pastor's wife called us for dinner. We crowded into the kitchen. I expected a simple meal of corn or beans and greens.

But I was wrong. Spread out before me was roast turkey, a freshly stewed chicken, new potatoes, three vegetables, fresh fruit, and a native sweet! How could I possibly "indulge" in the midst of such poverty? I felt a knot the size of a grapefruit in my stomach. In spite of myself, tears began to roll down my cheek.

I wept for me and the shame of my own unthankful heart. I wept for them, with their sorrows, heartaches, and struggle simply to survive. I wept for the sheer joy I experienced as I was warmed and blessed and filled with *their joy* in sharing with me.

For a moment, I had wanted to pull down the blinds so I wouldn't have to look at their poverty. Instead, I opened myself to their hospitality—and their joy in sharing because of my joy in receiving. Together we were blessed.

A faithful steward—faithful stewardship—means being ready to share all we possess. A wealthy New York tycoon wrote The Foundation Library Center asking them to list the top fifty gifts in all history. The person wanted to see the list and make a gift to top them.

The inquiry received the following response:
Sir:
I should like to nominate for place among your fifty largest gifts in history the two mites which a

lady in Palestine dropped into the collection box nearly two thousand years ago.

Perhaps you remember what an observer said at that time: "This poor widow has put in more than all those who are contributing to the treasury. For they all contributed out of their abundance; but she out of her poverty has put in everything she had, her whole living." Indeed, you might wish to place this gift at the head of the list. Certainly it is one of the largest in terms of capacity to pay. Besides, it has by the power of its example brought to philanthropy many, many millions of dollars, particularly from people of small income, who nowadays, even statistically, give "more than their all."

So often I have experienced that quality of giving. I think of the two dollars and eleven cents given to feed the poor, starving babies in Africa by four- and six-year-old sisters. It was all of their savings.

Then there was the check for more than $5,000, the gifts given to a grieving family who lost an only son in a tragic motorcycle accident. We used it to assist some of the "boat people" who had fled from Vietnam.

And the diamond ring . . . the only thing of value one lady possessed. But she sold it for the sake of those who had nothing.

A fourteenth-century Korean ceramic bowl—one family's priceless heirloom—was converted into cash to fill the bowls of several hundred children in an East Africa feeding program.

An expensive original painting, two valuable coin collections, and a choice lakeside vacation lot were all donated by a pulp-mill laborer . . . who received joy through divesting himself of unnecessary treasures . . . in order to better invest himself for Jesus' sake.

"Well done, good and faithful steward! You have been faithful with a few things; I will put you in charge of many things. Come and share your master's happiness!" (Matthew 25:23).

"Whoever wants to become great among you must be your servant, and whoever wants to be first must be slave of all" (Mark 10:43,44).

Chapter 10

Servant Leaders

*M*ortar shells screamed from the dark jungle. All night long the earth convulsed with explosions, the night sky hemorrhaging with horizon-wide flashes, freezing huddled groups of refugees into eerie black-and-white snapshots of terror. Panic ruled the night. Rumors shot through camp like white-hot shrapnel. Soldiers! Invasion! Rape! Genocide!

Nor were the rumors without justification. The hill overlooking this United Nations refugee camp on the border of Thailand had indeed fallen under the control of marauding Khmer Rouge forces.

More than 100,000 despairing Cambodian refugees knew what they could expect from the invaders. One more horror after years of horror. Blood upon blood, death upon death, sorrow upon sorrow.

Even when the camp had provided a fragile shelter, life had been cruelly difficult—a struggle for survival. Inadequate "longhouses" to shelter them against the monsoon rains, endless food lines, long hours of interviews with refugee officials, limited medical services for those who were diseased and dying—and now this.

Inside the bamboo-framed tent hospital, Dr. Jim Owens struggled for control. Dying patients were being snatched from hospital cots by terrified family members. Mothers ripped life-giving I.V. units from their children's emaciated arms and ran sobbing into the moonless night. They had suffered so long—in famine, in war. Memories of Pol Pot's blood-crazed army were seared into their minds. This overcrowded border refugee camp had offered a hope for security—a hope further shattered by each death-dealing rocket.

All night long Dr. Jim labored to quiet the patients, to reason with distraught parents, to assure the sick and dying of safety when he knew all too well that his own life was in jeopardy. But there was simply no other place of refuge to flee to. The doctor worked like six men—worked and prayed—until dawn came and the invasion force was driven back across the border by crack Thai army units.

BOOT CAMP FOR WORLD-CHANGERS!

Dr. Jim Owens, husband and father; Seattle-area physician; active churchman and community leader. What was it that would persuade an American doctor, securely established in a practice, to leave security and safety for a chaotic refugee camp? Dr. Jim had but one desire: to serve the suffering in Jesus' name in a place where the need was most critical and the opportunity to witness of his Christian faith most powerful.

Two days after the cross-border invasion, Jim took me around his primitive tent hospital. There was pride in his voice as he showed off some new additions and equipment. Compassion radiated from his face as he bent over the frail, sick bodies. He shared story after story with me as we walked, stories of lives saved and lives lost. But all the while his hands were constantly busy: an injection here, an I.V. needle into the arm of a starving baby, fresh dressing on the wounds of a new amputee, a cool cloth for a fevered brow.

We came to an eighteen-year-old refugee mother who sat

by her dying husband, cradling his head in her lap. Not even Dr. Jim had the courage to tell her that her undernourished baby had died during the night.

He chatted with a young boy and turned back to me with joy on his face. Everyone had given up hope that the child would live—everyone but Dr. Jim. Now the little boy had recovered, and could laugh and smile again.

Knowing Jim's medical resources back home in his Seattle practice, I could feel his pain when he would re-wrap the stump of a bomb-shattered leg, ladle simple gruel for a starving child, and provide the most basic medications to help ease the pain of a dying man.

Jim had left the easy life for an opportunity to serve others. He answered the call to "come change our world!" And he understood the upside-down values of Kingdom service.

Want to be great? *Become a servant.*

Want to be first? *Become a slave of all.* For eight months, Dr. Jim and his nurse/wife Ann lived out that challenge among the Cambodian refugees in Thailand. The Owens children were sent to a missionary kids' school in a neighboring country so Jim and Ann could pour all their energies into serving. For thirty-two weeks, a cramped room in a crowded native house substituted for their comfortable Seattle home.

And this was just a beginning of volunteer service for the Owenses. After their work in Indochina, Jim and Ann led the initial medical team in Camp Halba, a festering refugee camp in Somalia described by writer Philip Yancey as "the other side of hell."

During the early weeks of the program, they struggled day and night to stem the tide of disease and death among more than 45,000 refugees who fled the Ogaden Desert war in Ethiopia. Once again they ministered from a small tent, with primitive equipment and woefully inadequate medical supplies. During several months of selfless service, together with other members of a World Concern medical team, they were able to slow the death rate, care for the dying, and help heal the sick.

When bombs exploded all across Lebanon, Dr. Jim once again led a disaster relief medical team that helped bind up the wounds of the innocent victims of that tragic conflict. Jim's next assignment was back in Southeast Asia, at the World Vision administered pediatric hospital in Cambodia.

Christmas of 1984 found Jim in the midst of yet another crisis situation. University Presbyterian Church of Seattle commissioned him as their representative to the starving multitudes in Ethiopia. As of this writing Dr. Jim once again confronts human suffering with the compassionate skill of a caring healer.

Jim and Ann Owens understand—and practice—Christ's deceptively simple formula: Lose your life for Jesus and the sake of his gospel and—for the first time—you will begin to really find it.

Remote mountain clinics, disease-infested swamplands, chaotic refugee camps, and drought-stricken, famine-haunted villages are all great locations for training servant-leaders.

These are not the people who are motivated by money, possessed with power, or searching for acclaim and publicity. These are the ones who understand that the way to greatness is through service to others.

SERVICE IS THE RENT YOU PAY

Not long ago I spoke with Malcolm Muggeridge about the crushing needs of our broken world, and the opportunities for service this brings. I remember his saying to me, "You know, Art, service is the rent you pay for your space on this planet."

I like that!

It's far more than a pious platitude to confess that we are "saved to serve." Christ's offered salvation is not given just to rescue us from sin, but to equip us for Kingdom service. In that sense, salvation is not so much a prize to be won as it is a responsibility to be assumed.

Jesus Christ is perfect in his example, not only because he was free from sin but because he was absolutely selfless in how he ministered to others. Today he sends his church into the world to be a servant church.

A GOSPEL OF "FLESH AND BLOOD"

I've met these world-changers in scores of countries. Each of them is characterized by a zeal for Christ and by a keen desire to really *serve* others in his name.

My thoughts leap to men like John Sy Cip, a prominent Philippine-Chinese millionaire who became concerned for the poor of his world—the southern Philippine island of Mindanao. From his concern and vision the Philippine Evangelistic Enterprises was born, ministering to the physical and spiritual needs of rural farmers, city students, and remote tribal groups. In addition to promoting efforts in evangelism, education, and religious broadcasting, Mr. Sy Cip puts flesh and blood into the gospel of Christ by securing land rights for displaced tribal farmers, by providing medical services for the rural poor, and by developing farms and agricultural training programs.

I think of couples like Jean and Denny Grindell, successful Seattle-area florists who have spent half of every year for the past decade serving the Masai people in the Great Rift Valley in Kenya.

Dr. Archie and Huldah Fletcher come to mind. Born of missionary parents in Korea, they served the people of India for many years through the Miraj Medical Center, southeast of Bombay. When the time for retirement came, the Fletchers found a life of ease in America simply unacceptable.

The next time I crossed paths with them was in Kathmandu, Nepal. Archie directed the medical program at Shanta Bawan Hospital. Most recently they accepted a new "retirement" assignment in the Central African Republic—after months of intensive language study in Europe!

I first met Dr. Tess Ladrillo following a church service in Manila. Beautiful, gifted, and secure in her private practice, she inquired whether there were any places of service for her.

Months later she was on her way to Ban Vinai, one of the border refugee camps in Thailand. There, working long hours with very limited resources, she poured her gifts, energies, and heart into training dental paramedics among the refugee populace.

Deo and Elaine Miller, highly successful Southern California contractors, were first introduced to me in the lobby of one of Singapore's plushest hotels. They had gone to Sri Lanka on a "tropical paradise" vacation . . . but found their hearts broken in "Hell's Seventeen Acres." On just seventeen acres of land near the outskirts of Colombo, they found thousands of squatter families living in unspeakable poverty. Numb with despair, the people had virtually given up hope for a better future.

Some time later I visited this human dumping ground—with Deo and Elaine as my guides. They had exchanged a prosperous business and a comfortable Southern California hillside ranch house, complete with garden and swimming pool, for a cramped, hot flat in a Colombo apartment building. They spent their days developing cottage industries, vocational training opportunities, and feeding centers for the malnourished children. At night, they would dream and plan and scheme about how they might touch the lives of those beaten, defeated men, women, and children in Hell's Seventeen Acres.

Deo and Elaine understood the stakes. They knew what they were facing—crushed spirits, broken minds and bodies, entrenched evil and oppression, attitudes formed by generations of poverty, illiteracy, and malnutrition. It wasn't going to be easy. It wasn't going to be quick. It wasn't going to generate "positive press reports" in the churches back home. But they threw themselves into the work, body and soul, hearts as one, in Jesus' name.

Utilizing their skills and experiences, these servant-leaders developed and launched Sri Lanka Child-Care, an organization that is gradually bringing help and healing to this dark little corner of God's world.

It may still be "Hell's Seventeen Acres" . . . but a new resident is becoming known in the shanties, streets, and alleyways. A new face. A new force.

Its name is Hope.

WHO IS A SERVANT-LEADER?

Be careful how you pronounce "servant-leader." The emphasis is always upon *servant*. The other half of the title takes care of itself.

Servant-leaders attempt to influence, not control. They respond to the needs of others, rather than devoting their total energies to meeting their own needs.

I was sitting with a group of children in the dining room of a Christian vocational school in Ethiopia. Started by a missionary with vision and compassion, this ministry was now being carried forward by Ethiopian lay-leaders. That nation's Marxist-controlled central government still made provision for private initiative devoted to helping the homeless and disadvantaged children, many gathered from the streets of Addis Ababa.

Turning from my tea and biscuits, I noticed a motto on the wall—a slogan attributed to Martin Luther King, Jr.:

> In order to live
> creatively and
> meaningfully, our self-concern
> must be wedded to other-concern.

This is the starting point for servant-leaders. As Mother Teresa puts it: "We serve Him when we care for Him among the poor; we love Him best when we love those who need Him most."

The servant-leader is not one who nervously rushes about trying to redeem people or rescue them in their moments of extreme physical, social, or spiritual desperation. He is not a bundle of restless energy, a "do-gooder" who wanders the landscape in search of wrongs to right. Forget the Don Quixotic

knight who jousts with windmills for some intangible concept
of "glory."

Servant-leaders have a plan, a goal. They know what they
are about. Their consuming passion is to affirm the Good News
of Jesus Christ. They know that by serving others, their very
lives declare that there is something about God that every man
and woman needs to confront and understand . . . that this God
whom they serve is LOVE . . . that God's Son has come to roll
back the darkness and despair . . . that life can be changed
forever by embracing his powerful Name.

In his book, *The Wounded Healer,* Henri Nouwen writes:

> Behind every painful symptom of suffering, there is
> a loving Savior who is ready to heal, to bring hope to
> the hopeless, life for the dying, cleansing to those
> leprous from the stain and pain of this life. . . . It is
> only the compassionate servant who is able to dis-
> cern symptoms from solutions, to break through the
> vicious cycle of immediate needs demanding im-
> mediate solutions, and direct the weary, the suffer-
> ing, the broken to the only One who can bring rest.

A WILLINGNESS TO DRAW NEAR

Until we are ready to take on the hurts and sorrows of those
we intend to serve, we will not be recognized as servant-leaders.

You can't really do that from a "safe distance."

You can't live out your whole life in a comfortable,
sanitized, hermetically sealed environment and say that you
have truly become Christ's presence to a dying world. If the
closest you ever come to the poor and oppressed is within the
pages of your Time magazine or within proximity of your televi-
sion set during famine shots from Africa on the CBS Evening
News . . . it isn't likely that you'll go very far beyond pity. And
pity doesn't bring much help to anyone.

Think for a moment of the Lord Jesus. He could have
healed the leper in Matthew 8 with a word—or a silent com-

mand—or the blink of his eye. Instantly. At a distance. Instead, he "reached out his hand and touched the man" (v. 3). He cared enough to get close; he loved enough to draw near.

A servant-leader, like his Lord, is willing to draw near. To see, to smell, to touch, to listen, to empathize. To look eye to eye, to touch hand to hand. "Drawing near" might take you around the world. Then again it might take you down-state, across town . . . or next door. It's a cinch it will take you *out* of the easy chair, *out* of the warm assurance of your four protective walls, and most likely *out* of your "comfort zone."

Out is the key word. An uncomfortable word, to be sure, but the beginning place for true ministry, true servant-leadership. Jesus had another word for it . . . no less comfortable, no less directional.

The word he used is . . . *go*.

To Lead Is to Dream

An ability to foresee the unforeseeable is yet another mark of the servant-leader. Foresight is the "lead" in the word "leader." Visionary leadership is the ability to know what is going to happen when the future becomes part of the present. When the leader loses vision he is no longer leading, but only reacting.

Nothing great ever happens without a great dream.

I think back to an evening when the telephone rang beside my bed in a hotel room. The warm, raspy voice on the line was Dr. Mark Buntain, missionary pastor of Calcutta's Assembly of God Church. I invited him up to my room.

Mark was dreaming dreams that night . . . dreams for a servant ministry to the people of Calcutta.

I listened, and I watched. His voice rose, and with every rise in inflection there was a growing intensity in his eyes. Mark dreamed of a Christian hospital to treat the ills of his beloved people: not an ordinary hospital, but a research center complete with a nursing school. He could close his eyes and see compassionate, professional, centralized medical care—with mobile clinics and outreach medical stations in the various suburbs of Calcutta.

He dreamed of schools and churches, of feeding programs for hungry children, and of vocational training programs for unemployed moms and dads.

The intensity in his voice rose to a raspy crescendo—his eyes lighting up the dim Calcutta hotel room like twin torches—as he sketched out a marvelous vision of what could be for these dear, impoverished people. To me it was only a vision, but to Mark . . . to Mark it was already a reality.

INSPIRED BY EXAMPLE

Through the years I've had the opportunity to observe first-hand the wide-reaching ministry of the Buntains, now called Calcutta's Mission of Mercy.

One of my first encounters with Mark was late one night in the middle of a raging monsoon. He had just picked me up at Calcutta's International Airport. As we drove through those dark, flooded streets and narrow alleys, I began to see that the night's agenda would be a little more involved than a quick trip to my hotel. At the end of one narrow road, Pastor Buntain pulled up to a stop and told me to wait in the truck. "When you can't see me anymore," he said as he jumped out, "turn off the headlights."

I watched him wade out into the darkness. One moment he was moving waist-deep in the sewage-filled water, and then he was gone. I turned off the lights and waited.

A small boat slipped by the car. I could hear voices calling for help from the rooftops of nearby houses. I waited and prayed.

Thirty minutes later I was startled when the truck door opened. Mark slipped back into the truck, started the engine, and without a word turned the vehicle around and headed for the high ground of Airport Road.

When I pressed him for an explanation, Mark told me that he was delivering funds from the church to help those made homeless by the floods. His tone was so matter-of-fact. Just another "normal" day in the life of this unusual servant-leader.

Pastor Buntain is a leader—no doubt about that—but his leadership springs from the *example of his life*. His life of selfless service to others has inspired thousands all over the world and has brought credibility to a gospel that declares "God is love" to a violent, impoverished, and oppressive society so seldom touched by love.

DREAMS THAT BRING LIFE

This was the Mark Buntain who dreamed such wonderful—and audacious—dreams.

I remember their joy as they introduced me to Andy, a fat and happy one-year-old. He had been given up a few months before by his desperate mother. Wrapped only in a filthy rag, little Andy had been starving, his frail body racked by disease and very near to death. His mother had lost her milk . . . and with it, all hope. She had nothing. No husband, no home, no shelter, no food. Severely malnourished herself, she knew only too well that keeping her baby would only bring death to both of them.

Andy was brought into the busy walk-up apartment which served as the Buntains' parsonage. Their little flat was already too crowded, but baby Andy was taken right in. You might say he was swept up into the Buntains' dreams . . . a dream that he could be nourished back to health, a dream that so many others just like him would be saved through one church's daring rescue plan.

Today that dream stands complete—a medical center nine stories tall! Just as Mark Buntain visualized in my hotel room, the hospital conducts important medical research, trains nurses, and administers a mobile clinic that makes its regular rounds from one outpatient clinic to another. At the same time, thousands of children are nourished daily through the church's feeding programs.

Happy little Andy is a warm, bright-eyed, huggable representation of a servant-leader's "dreams." Today he lives a full life in Sweden with his newly adopted parents.

"NOT A SHOWCASE, BUT A PATTERN"

The exemplary life of servant-leadership will accomplish far more than all of our theological formulations, development philosophies, and leadership models.

In the 1920s and 30s, Dr. Y. C. Yan successfully tested certain principles of community development in what was known as the Ting Hsien Experiment. These principles have been adopted as a credo for the International Institute for Rural Reconstruction in the Philippines.

> Go to the poor.
> Live among the poor.
> Learn from the poor.
> Work with the poor.
> Start with what the poor have and
>   build upon what the poor possess.
> Teach by showing; learn by doing.
> Not a showcase, but a pattern;
> Not odds and ends, but a system.
> Not piecemeal, but integrated;
> Not to conform, but to transform;
> Not relief, but release.

The validity of our Lord's example has not diminished in almost 2,000 years. To be master is to become servant of all. We should not so much seek to follow in his footsteps as to seek what he sought.

"For you know the grace of our Lord Jesus Christ, that though he was rich, yet for your sakes he became poor, so that you through his poverty might become rich" (2 Corinthians 8:9).

A CALL TO COMMITMENT

A couple of years ago, two World Concern team members serving in Bangladesh had to return home to the Philippines for the funeral of a family member. Deng and Sucel Samonte had given up successful professional careers for the sake of Christ to serve among the thousands of displaced poor in Dhaka.

Sucel's brother Edgar had chosen another path of service, a path which led ultimately to violence and death. As a leader of the Communist party in the Philippines, he was killed in a military ambush.

But both sister and brother had desired to serve the poor and oppressed. Tragically, Edgar's method to effect change relied on violence. And yet each shared a burning desire to make the world better, more just, more responsive to human need.

Reflecting on the meaning of her brother's death, Sucel wrote me a letter.

"Edgar turned away from self," she wrote, "and committed himself to a goal of making poor people better off than what they are now. He gave all his talents, all his time, all of his little resources to be used toward that goal.

"As Jesus Christ's follower, God has commanded me to turn away from self. If God chooses to put me in a [life-threatening] situation, would I be as selfless as Edgar was?"

She closes her letter with some tough questions about life, its meaning, its values. Then she asks, "Was Edgar an atheist? I don't know. But if indeed he was an atheist, what does that mean for me, who has access to God's love? Doesn't God expect from me greater love, greater selflessness, greater commitment?

"Love, selflessness, commitment to a cause—Edgar had all of these. As a Christian do I have these qualities, too?"

Searching questions. Questions we would do well to ponder as we invest the remaining hours, days, and years God has graciously allowed to each of us. I may spend my life serving others for Jesus' sake, or I may spend my life serving myself.

But the bottom line says I can only spend it once.

"All the believers were together. . . . they gave to anyone as he had need. . . . they continued to meet together. . . . They broke bread in their homes and ate together with glad and sincere hearts, praising God and enjoying the favor of all the people. And the Lord added to their numbers daily those who were being saved" (Acts 2:44-47).

Chapter 11

Redemptive Communities

*T*he sun rose like a fiery ball over the flat desert country of Somalia. At first it was only a faint light on the eastern horizon. Small touches of color began to appear in wispy clouds overhead. Bright fingers of blazing glory seemed to radiate out from the desert floor. Then . . . the merest cap of the sun itself. As it slipped upward I could feel its warmth begin to remove the chill of the clear desert night. That welcome warmth would soon become a burning heat—turning the daytime desert into an oven.

I sat by the banks of the Juba river, pondering this glorious exhibition, wondering if it was a parable with a larger meaning.

Where once there had been the chilling night of war and famine—a refugee community living on the edge of terror and desperation—this had all changed. The Son had come to Halba, bringing light, warmth, and life.

I remembered the first night I had come to Camp Halba. It was both literally and figuratively in the middle of the night. The moonlight revealed the unmistakable mounds of east African *mondals,* the small, spherical houses made from sticks intricately woven into an inverted bowl and covered with thorn bush and discarded paper. When daylight came, I discovered that many of the frames were not covered at all. The occupants, like thousands of others who lay out under the black desert sky, were exposed to the cold of the night with no shelter, no covering. The stillness of the night was broken only by the distant wail of a mother and her female friends mourning one more needless death of a starving child. When dawn came the frail, lifeless body would be laid out in a row with others and covered with stones. Stones were plentiful in Halba. So were graves.

I remembered how grim life appeared that first morning. More than 45,000 refugees having fled the terror of war now faced the specter of starvation, disease, and slow death in a desolate camp far from home. Days went by with no food. Emergency supplies, when they did come, were tragically meager. Scores died every day, mostly children. They died from hunger and they died from disease—diseases easily preventable under normal conditions.

But Halba has entered a new day. Enormous changes have transformed its once hopeless face. People no longer die from hunger. Children have now been inoculated against the childhood diseases. Tuberculosis has been brought under control, and its victims are now receiving treatment. Farmers, former desert nomads, rise early to till their fields and tend their tall rows of ripening corn. Women bend over small mud-brick stoves, no longer needing to despoil the environment by burning the precious thorn bushes and ground cover in inefficient open fires. Trained refugee paramedics busy themselves with the care of those who seek medical assistance. The American refugee-worker crew chief heads out with his team of laborers to work on half-finished irrigation canals which will direct the precious waters of a nearby river through acre after acre of sun-scorched earth.

The desert will bloom. Fields of green vegetables and rippling grain will welcome each new sunrise.

BEARERS OF THE SON

What has made all the difference? How has a disaster relief camp become such a redemptive community?

I thought of the "pioneers" as I reflected that bright morning on the banks of the gentle Juba . . . that new breed of missionaries entering service for their Lord: Christian doctors, nurses, social workers, nutritionists, handymen, drivers, and agriculturists.

I thought of "Golden-hands," a mechanical genius from the Netherlands. I thought of Ria and Oetje, skilled and compassionate nurses who had come with him. There were Joey and Lita, medical professionals from the Philippines . . . and so many more. A cook from America, an engineer from Canada, a midwife from England, a pharmacist from Korea. With keen minds, extensive training, a zeal born out of compassion for the poor and oppressed—and the love of Jesus burning in their souls—they came to bring hope and health, nurture and nutrition to these refugees who had suffered so much.

An impoverished refugee camp had been changed into a redemptive community. Prayers to the true and living God rose to the skies from humble mondals. Weekly Bible studies and sharing groups brought many into new understanding—and new life. There wasn't a "church planter" or "evangelist" among the whole cadre of Christian workers; the rigid laws of this Islamic nation forbid such open Christian activity. Yet the witness was unmistakable, quiet and strong, compassionate and sure. Thousands of Somalians were exposed to the reality of God's love. Jesus Christ became "flesh" once again through the loving actions of redeemed change agents.

Camp Halba, once accurately described as "the other side of hell," had tasted a bit of heaven.

A FLICKER OF HOPE AT "WORLD'S END"

The Mathari Valley of Kenya lies hundreds of miles to the south and west of Halba. If the residents of that valley were to run a "for sale" ad in your local newspaper, it might include a line like this: *Close to major commercial and business center for all of East Africa . . . within miles of high-rise hotels and modern convention center.*

That's true. The valley lies within sight of the Nairobi skyline. Trouble is, no one who knew better would even want to get close to the Mathari Valley, let alone buy it. This is not Kenya's fabled Great Rift Valley with its abundant wildlife and colorful tribal people. No, the Mathari is something else. You almost expect a sign to greet you with a message like: "Welcome to the End of the Earth."

It is a place of brokenness, of mind-staggering poverty, of physical and spiritual ruin. Dreadful paper shacks crowd each other for space on the valley's steep slopes. Narrow, muddy streets lined with open sewers wind through small openings beside endless rows of shanties. In all the world I cannot remember seeing men and women as incredibly impoverished or emotionally depressed. More than fifty percent of its women and girls are prostitutes. Their alternatives are very few.

One hundred fifty thousand people pinioned by chains of corruption and deprivation as binding as those of cold steel.

But a flower blooms in the midst of Mathari's misery. A redemptive community has come to the valley. As a "shining light on the hill," its brilliance has penetrated the darkness, its warmth dispelling the coldness of fear, hopelessness, and despair. Bishop Kitanga, a gifted and visionary servant-leader, and a compassionate body of believers are in the process of bringing transformation to the lives and futures of the Mathari Valley people.

What an incredible flood of joy washed over me as I worshiped with these glad-hearted brothers and sisters in Christ. Following a one-hour Bible lesson by the pastor, I was invited to give a forty-minute "missionary call." The singing was punctuated by full-voiced "Amens" and "Hallelujahs." A New Orleans-type trombonist led the happy crowds in their praises. African drums beat out rhythms which spoke of deliverance rather than bondage.

More than a thousand worshipers jammed the aisles, filled the seats, and crowded the openings of every window and door, while a crackling P.A. system broadcast the joyful sounds to thousands more who could listen from a distance.

"I know where you live," the Son of God wrote to the church at Pergamum, *"where Satan has his throne.* Yet you remain true to my name" (Revelation 2:13). The letter could have been written to the church of Mathari. For surely if Satan moved his throne from ancient Pergamum, he would have found this wretched valley a likely site to relocate. *What was it then,* in the midst of such festering poverty—poverty of mind, body, and spirit—that created such an environment of joy, hope, and deliverance? Why had this new group of believers mushroomed to such size, several thousand scattered around the valley in six congregations?

The secret didn't take long to discern. *Changed lives!* Prostitutes were being set free from the economic slavery of the world's oldest profession. Ruthless money-lenders had been forgiven and freed from their oppressive ways. Street-thieves were now trusting Christ and helpful Christian friends for assistance rather than robbing by day and thieving by night.

After the service, the Bishop and his elders led me on a tour of the valley. We looked in on the church's carpentry shops. We toured an impressive leather-making factory with its purses, belts, bags, and book covers attractively displayed on hand-crafted counters. We stopped by the church's clinic, whose services included care for nursing mothers and children under age five.

Fresh breezes whisper among the shanties of the forlorn valley . . . a thousand demonstrations of brotherhood drive back the bitter gloom. Here is a wonder. Here is hope and caring and grace and healing. Here is the Church of Jesus Christ, God's redeemed and redemptive community, making its presence seen and heard and felt.

The flower blooming in Mathari is beautiful beyond description. Its blossom is hardy. Its fragrance is reaching around the world.

The Church as God's redemptive community gains its credence not through glass cathedrals, massive budgets, and impressive strategies, but through its loving incarnational witness to those who despair.

SISTERS OF MARY MAGDALENE

Aling Maria discovered a redemptive community. She may have found it half a lifetime too late, but still, she found it.

A young Filipino pastor introduced me to Aling Maria during my most recent visit to his country. Aling and Pastor Pantoja were struggling together to find a way to bring Christ's redemptive message to the prostitutes of Olangapo.

Aling Maria knew what that life was like.

For fourteen years she had been the mistress of a wealthy Filipino man. He had promised to marry her—but never did. Aling Maria clung to the relationship through the birth of three children, always hoping that one day she could be given the dignity and security of marriage.

One day, in a drunken stupor her "man" hacked off the arm of a fellow drinking companion in a barroom brawl. He was thrown into prison by the local police. Aling Maria had no means of supporting the young children. In her desperation, she took up the life of a prostitute. For this, in time she too was imprisoned. When released, knowing that her life was at a dead-end, she gathered the three children and a few personal possessions, boarded a local bus, and headed off to the big city—Manila—where she hoped to find a new opportunity.

On the outskirts of her small provincial town, the bus was abruptly stopped by a group of village people. Her three children were forcibly dragged from the bus by relatives of her common-law husband. "You can leave," they informed Aling Maria, "but you cannot take the children with you."

Her voice broke as she told me, "That's the last time I ever saw my children."

Aling Maria could find no employment in Manila, so she

did what so many young women in third world countries do: She headed to the best town she could find to practice the trade of prostitution.

Work wasn't hard to find in Olangapo, the Filipino city that adjoins Subic Bay, the largest overseas U.S. Naval base. Prostitution thrives to meet the passions and the appetites of American sailors on shore leave. There are 16,000 government-licensed prostitutes in Subic Bay—and two unlicensed prostitutes for every legal one.

Snaking its way through the middle of the city, Magsaysay Avenue is lined with go-go and strip joints, cabarets, bars, and cheap hotels. The neon lights are bright and gaudy. Rock music blares from every doorway. The avenue offers every form of sexual perversion you've ever heard of—and many you would not want to know about. It is an unbelievable cesspool of human degradation.

Eighty-five percent of the city's 48,000 prostitutes speak either *Boholano* or *Wari-Wari,* the languages of the most impoverished areas of the Philippines. This underscores the fact that for the woman of the third world, prostitution is not a sexual choice—but a forced economic decision. Families send their daughters into prostitution as the only means of putting bread on the table.

For fourteen years Aling Maria plied her trade. Demonstrating real business acumen and management skill, she rose to become "madam" of one of Subic Bay's most prosperous cabarets, where she managed a retinue of more than fifty bar girls. She made a great deal of money for the owners of the business, but her life became increasingly unlivable. The load of her own personal sin weighed heavy on her spirit. She controlled the lives and destinies of fifty young women—girls as impoverished and desperate as she had been in those early years.

Then she met Danny Pantoja, once a student radical but now the concerned pastor of a local Baptist church. Pastor Danny introduced Aling Maria to the love and cleansing power of Jesus Christ. Weary of her degraded, debauched life, she gladly received God's forgiveness and became a new creature in Christ.

As I sat in the pastor's crowded *sala,* hearing Aling Maria's story, I was impressed with the beauty of Christ upon her face. She was stout and middle-aged now. The bloom of her youth was gone. Years of rough living had etched hard lines in her face. Yet nothing could stop the glow of a cleansed heart and a Christ-filled spirit from shining through.

Together, Aling Maria, Pastor Danny, and I planned and dreamed of a program to help reach the prostitutes of Subic Bay. These girls, called wayward by so many, are only looking for a decent option in life. Assuredly they need the forgiveness of sin that only Christ can bring. But it is *economic opportunity* that will enable them to restructure a life of purity and respectability.

Even as I write these words, we're busy at work, doing some preliminary dreaming and planning on the development of a new *carinderia,* a low-cost Filipino fast food restaurant on Magsaysay Avenue. For *this* avenue, it will be an eatery with a radical difference. No booze, no lustful men. Instead, a clean, quiet atmosphere where Aling Maria and others can reach out a hand of love and friendship to girls who crave another chance— another option.

The new *carinderia* could very well house the first Baptist religious order! We would call it the Sisters of Mary Magdalene. It would be a redemptive community limited only to former prostitutes. We're visualizing a sorority-type initiation rite where the young women would deliberately set their old lives behind. The girls will wear uniforms of pure white (uniforms are very Filipino) with an embroidered logo of a pile of stones, to remind them—and others—of the stones that were set aside when the woman caught in adultery was brought before the Lord Jesus. The emblem will serve another purpose, too. When people ask, "What do those stones mean?" these forgiven women will find an opportunity to speak of the One who brings new life . . . and second chances.

THE SERVING COMMUNITY

"An excellent way to size up a religion," writes Dr. Kenneth Scott, "is to look at its response toward human suffering and need."

The Buddhist says of suffering, "Forget it. These problems exist only in your mind. Pay no attention to them."

The Muslim says, "It is Allah's will. Suffering is inevitable. Don't resist it."

The Hindu says, "You deserve it. It's what's coming to you. You should try harder in the next reincarnation."

The Christian response, Scott rightly observes, has to be different. The Christian says, "God loves you and I do, too. Let me do what I can to help you." He does this remembering the words of his Lord: "Whatever you did for one of the least of these brothers of mine, you did for me" (Matthew 25:40).

As caring communities, we have a very special responsibility to serve others. Paul tells the Christians scattered throughout Galatia that they were not to become "weary in doing good," but rather, "as we have opportunity, let us do good to all people, especially to those who belong to the family of believers" (Galatians 6:9, 10).

Opportunities? You can't compute them! They are as innumerable as human needs. Yet all too often the eroding forces of negativism, cynicism, and apathy have sent precious opportunities begging—and have banished Christians into an unsatisfying, ingrown, self-centered life-style.

Certain groups of Christians would rather romanticize the sweet bye and bye instead of realistically confronting the nasty now and now.

Other groups of believers bemoan closed doors to the gospel of Jesus Christ around the world. Closed doors? It's a myth! There are no closed doors, only closed minds which are blind to new methods, new approaches, and new opportunities—closed hearts which refuse to believe the promises of God. "I have placed before you an open door," says our Lord, "that no one can shut" (Revelation 3:8).

With these opportunities before us, then, we are to be a caring, serving community. The call is to do our deeds of mercy for all. But we are admonished to remember our special responsibility to the family of believers.

ENRICHED BY SERVING

Coleen was tired.

The tropical sun beat down relentlessly on the small, rocky island three miles off the coast of Malaysia. Her task would have been a difficult one under any circumstances—the oppressive heat only made it that much harder. Coleen was teacher, mother, counselor, and companion to several hundred "unaccompanied minors," bright, active children from ages two to fifteen who had arrived on this refugee island by frail boats. All of the children had endured torturous, dangerous journeys from the shores of their native Vietnam. Some had made the voyage in six days. Others had journeyed for six weeks. It all depended upon the weather, the seas, and the number of attacks by the merciless Thai pirates.

Nguyen had been shoved aboard a departing boat by a concerned adult friend. The five-year-old boy was alone in the world. His mother had died in childbirth, his father was imprisoned in a Communist "reeducation camp." He was scared and lonely, wondering what would happen to him or if anyone would help him and care for him. Nguyen's young mind, made old by seeing the suffering of others, longed for the settled days of his earlier childhood. But now the long-house was home for him and hundreds of other children just like him.

During daytime hours, Coleen organized games to occupy the children. In the evenings she labored patiently with those who were struggling to learn English. At night it was difficult to sleep. The camp never slept. All day long raucous loudspeakers droned out meeting announcements, names of new arrivals, lists of departing refugees, and summons for weary camp staffers. Filth, frustration, and sleeplessness seemed to be the primary ingredients of life in this teeming camp, or at least it seemed so to a one-day visitor like me.

"How does anyone live in this mad atmosphere day after day?" I asked.

With a weary smile, Coleen told me that she wouldn't trade her work on Pulau Bidong for any experience in her life. "I'm having the time of my life," she said.

Here is the Spirit of Christ in a serving community! In God's kingdom we are committed to community: bearing one another's burden, interdependence rather than independence. The good news is that *I am* my brother's keeper. We receive this responsibility as an opportunity, not an obligation. By giving away my life to others, I find life returning to me in far greater measure. The focus of the redeemed life is not found in the pursuit of materialism, individualism, and power, but in serving the needy, caring for the homeless and the oppressed, and in relinquishing personal power in order to become servant to the powerless. Coleen McGoff, student worker from Seattle, ten thousand miles from home, was learning the reality of Saint Francis's prayer:

> Lord, grant I may seek rather
>> to comfort than to be comforted;
>> to understand than to be understood;
>> to love than to be loved;
> for it is by forgetting self
>> that one finds,
> it is by forgiving
>> that one is forgiven,
> it is by dying
>> that one awakens to eternal life.

THE HEALING COMMUNITY

I was wandering through the half-destroyed air terminal in Guatemala City. Just a few score hours before, a gigantic earthquake had devastated this small but beautiful land of fiery volcanoes, sleepy Indian villages, and thick-carpeted jungles. The whole nation was in shock. More than 25,000 of its citizens had perished in a moment. Entire cities and towns lay in ruins.

Just as I passed the door to customs, I looked up and immediately noticed a friendly face in the crowd.

Dr. Raymond Benson, intently searching for his baggage, stood just a few feet away from me. Dr. Benson was a prominent Billings, Montana, surgeon and a former president of the American College of Surgeons. I knew of his selfless labor as a volunteer medical doctor in the hill country of Vietnam.

Clearing customs, we hurried together to attend a meeting called by local evangelical leaders to coordinate the massive relief effort. Afterwards, we went together to render what assistance we could to one of the devastated villages. We were greeted at the edge of the village by row upon row of freshly dug graves—silent witnesses to the massive destruction we would encounter within. We did what we could, distributing food and clearing rubble. Dr. Benson ministered to the medical needs of survivors.

We returned to the city late that night, sharing one of the scarce hotel rooms. We sat up late. The trauma of suffering and tragedy made it difficult to sleep. As we talked, I began to probe Dr. Benson's call to service.

"Art," he said, "I am a doctor. But I am a doctor who is also a Christian. And my understanding of Christ's call in my life is not merely that I behave as a Christian while I provide medical services. The medical profession is my avocation. My vocation is to witness of my faith in the Lord Jesus Christ through my medical skills. That's what brings me to Guatemala today."

This commitment to healing men's physical *and* spiritual diseases has led Dr. Benson and his Medical Ambassadors all over the face of the globe. Wherever they go, these medical missionaries are a *healing community* to the sick, the discouraged, and the dying.

It is not the Christian professional's task to race nervously around the globe trying to redeem people—to save them at that final moment before death. It is rather to constantly affirm one's commitment to the "good news" in Jesus Christ.

The gospels witness to the healing power of Jesus again and again: the lame made to walk, the blind to see, and the deaf to hear. But the Great Healer went further still: the lonely were comforted, the moral reprobates were forgiven, the harlot was cleansed, and the cheating tax-collector was transformed to live a life of service to others. The healing community is one where the poor can see, touch, smell, and hear the presence and power of the living Christ.

REDEEMED COMMUNITIES

Our immediate surroundings will always block out spiritual realities unless and until we encounter another human being whose living presence and witness to hope can challenge the emptiness and hopelessness of our own situation. It is this incarnational touch, this flesh-and-blood encounter with wholeness that brings healing. This encounter has the greatest potential and integrity when it comes through the hands of a wounded healer. For how can we possibly give leadership in caring ministries until we become willing to "take upon us" the poverty, the suffering, the despair of another?

It is always lonely to be surrounded by the sick and dying, the hungry and the hurting. We feel we have so little to give. But it is in that very act of giving, often from our own poverty, that we begin to catch a glimpse of a whole new dimension to life. As we are rubbed raw by the pain of others, we become aware of our own healing gifts—gifts we never even dreamed that we possessed. As never before, we find ourselves free to love and be loved, to breathe and eat and drink and feel like a person who has just realized he is really alive.

We cannot, however, give this wholeness to another person. *We can only create the safe and secure environment where the healing can take place.* It is here that redeemed communities become "the Balm in Gilead that heals the sin-sick soul."

It is not the healing community's task to remove human misery and pain. The very act of *sharing* pain with the distressed begins to create an environment where wholeness can be discovered. The Christian development worker, individually or in community, can never by his own actions remove all the causes of pain and suffering. It is pretentious to think we can. But in confronting those real causes of pain, as wounded healers we can become a guide to the hurting ones, a glint of hope for those on the verge of giving up. Our own humility and vulnerability offer a safe common ground for the sufferer to enter into that wholeness he senses in the healer. Sharing our hurts, our pain, and our failures, we find in time an opportunity to begin sharing our health. The impoverished man or woman begins to catch a vision . . . something shimmering on the dark horizon . . . a vision of wholeness . . . a vision of hope and healing and new life. Life can be different. There is something—Someone— beyond the pain and grief and emptiness. A hand reaches out. Another hand reaches back. And heaven smiles.

It has always been of great interest and encouragement for me to discover the healing process in a refugee camp. In the earliest days of a crisis, the primary instrument for healing is the professional relief worker. With a deep sense of caring and commitment, that seasoned worker responds with an overwhelming desire to assist those who suffer most where resources are least. But often it is not long until small communities of Christian refugees begin to form. Because of their own pain and suffering, these fellow refugees understand far better the feelings of desolation, fear, and hopelessness. They are able to reach out in authentic ways of healing. They can understand far more profoundly the feelings of the terrified new arrivals.

The nearly trained refugee paramedic delivers a level of health services far more personal and appropriate than the best-trained, most highly committed Westerner.

Developing Redeemed Communities

There are two things in life one cannot do alone—be married and be a Christian! It is easy for us to understand the marriage part of that statement, but in a day of highly individualized religious experience, we are liable to forget the second part of the equation. All too often we forget that becoming a Christian does more than put us into relationship with the "head," the Lord Jesus Christ; it also puts us into relationship with his redeemed people, the "body." We belong to the body as surely as we belong to the head.

The prophet Amos reminded the people of Israel of their very special relationship with Jehovah: "You only have I chosen of all the families of the earth . . ." But the prophet had another reminder: "Do two walk together unless they have agreed to do so?" (Amos 3:2, 3). In a day when privatization of faith is more characteristic of American Christianity than is shared community responsibility, it is essential to understand that the Church's call to community is *mandatory*—not optional. It can be no other way if the Church is to maintain its integrity in a divided and hurting world.

If the sense of community with the world-wide "household of faith" is lost, the essential character of the Church becomes violated. A western Christian church enjoying its affluence in a world where large communities of believers live in absolute poverty is a scandal to the gospel—a denial of our oneness in Christ.

Dom Helder Camara, the renowned bishop of Recife, Brazil, told his fellow members of the Vatican Council of his eagerness to see the entire church go boldly "in search of her lost poverty." Small in stature but large in heart, the bishop looked intently around the table at his ecclesiastical colleagues and admonished them with some inescapable historical data: "Before undertaking reforms," said Dom Helder, "the Church has always had to come to terms with her poverty."

Nowhere is the integrity of the Church as redeemed and

redemptive community more sorely tested than at the point of her voluntary impoverishment for the sake of bearing one another's burdens and sharing each other's resources. Will we indeed "bear one another's burdens, and so fulfill the law of Christ"? Or will we flinch under our Lord's scrutiny and walk away sad of heart like the rich young ruler? Purity of doctrine will not be the only agenda item when we stand before the judgment seat of Christ. The church at Ephesus had purity of doctrine, but they were rebuked by the glorified Christ for their lack of love.

The Church needs to return to basics. George Sweeting, president of Moody Bible Institute, states, "In this new day of awareness, godliness is inseparable from service to the poor. The Word of God teaches that God will bless those who reach out to help the poor. On the other hand, we literally invite God's judgment if we ignore these needs. . . . The question is not whether the church should help the poor, but how."

John Stott, chaplain to the Queen of England and former rector of All Souls Church, puts it like this: "If there is one community in the world in which justice is secured for the poor and need is eliminated, this should be the church."

In order to achieve such an expression of community, it is essential that we come to grips with both the nature and the strategy of the task our Lord has placed before us. What then, is the job description for a *redemptive community?*

> We must share in a stated purpose which is consistent with God's call upon his redeemed people and is fully accepted as the personal responsibility of each member of the community.
>
> This lofty purpose must be supported by measurable goals. Without measuring our progress, we cannot possibly achieve any goal.
>
> There must be both an identified and supported leadership, as well as a deeply committed and responsive "follow-ship."

An adequate organizational structure must follow—a plan which will help each community member to develop strategies for reaching the goal and will also provide an accountability structure essential for the discipline and unity of the body.

The Church has no shortage of fervent, Spirit-filled individuals ready to do the work of the kingdom. But without the gathering of these individuals into focused and disciplined communities, the scattered fires are dissipated in the cold darkness of overwhelming need. So often we spend our energies trying to sell people who are already sold rather than gathering, equipping, and sending them forth to accomplish what they are already motivated to do.

Bishop Festo Kivengere, an Anglican pastor from Uganda, saw this "scattered fire" as the principle reason for so much discouragement and failure in the ministry of serving the poor. When we serve alone rather than united in community we become overwhelmed before we've even begun.

The poet Ralph Waldo Emerson captured this idea when he wrote:

> What lies behind us
>   and What lies before us
> Are tiny compared to
>   What lies within us.

What lies within us is altogether incomplete and insufficient when isolated from the gifts and insights of the group. Together we can accomplish what any number of us individually could never accomplish alone. Here the service of small things becomes enlarged into mighty deeds and acts of mercy. In Christian community, simple assistance swells into a mighty tide. The shared insights, interlocking gifts, and unified witness of a redeemed community become the Spirit-driven force to effect change in environments of human impoverishment and resistance. It is here that

Like a mighty army
Moves the Church of God.

As World Concern's theology of development states, a redeemed community is called to be:

a *community* of worship in an age of the exaltation of man;

a *community* of loving servanthood in a world that enshrines self-seeking;

a *community* of brotherhood and reconciliation in a world torn by misunderstandings and fragmented by factions;

a *community* of relationships where our fraternity in Christ supersedes ties of nationalism, race, culture, clan, or family;

a *community* of unconditional liability for the spiritual, social, and economic needs of others;

a *community* of responsible stewardship in an age of consumption, waste, and extravagance;

a *community* of peace, creatively using nonviolence and peacemaking as a community vocation in an era of escalating violence and massive arms buildup;

a *community* of prophetic witness in an age increasingly influenced by humanism, secularism, and materialism;

a *community* of liberation from all forms of spiritual, physical, and social bondage;

a *community* committed to seeking first the manifestation of God's Kingdom in this darkened world . . . placing that mission before career, security, family, relationships, possessions, and even personal survival . . . believing fully that God will provide for those who will place his Kingdom first.

Caught up in the Spirit, the apostle John saw before him a throne in heaven. Seated upon the throne was the Lamb. Around the throne were those who sang a new song, saying:

> "You are worthy . . . because you were slain, and with your blood you purchased men for God from every tribe and language and people and nation."

The Lord Jesus paid the price to redeem. It is now our responsibility, as his very body, to become that redemptive *community* which bears witness to the truth, authenticates the "good news," redeems the sinner, liberates the oppressed, comforts the sorrowing, and sets the captive free.

The price of our redemption was costly. We dare not take our own redemptive responsibilities lightly.

"They . . . ate together with glad and sincere hearts. . . . And the Lord added to their number daily" (Acts 2:46, 47).

Chapter 12

Celebrating Saints

*O*ur first Christmas away from home!
It was all so disorienting to spend Christmas in the Philippines. Palm trees swayed gently in the tropical breeze outside our window . . . no substitute for a Douglas fir Christmas tree! The pungent odors of dried fish and chopped garlic simmering in large, smoke-blackened pots over open fires replaced the more familiar aromas of roasting turkeys, baking fruitcakes, and bubbling, spiced eggnogs.

These new smells of Christmas just wouldn't do!

Everything was different. We were used to enjoying a small, potted poinsettia in the middle of our festive Christmas table. This year the whole south side of our house was shaded by poinsettias standing fifteen feet tall!

The hot, humid weather hung like a soggy blanket around our bodies, day and night. There were no soft, falling snowflakes to fill the air with magic. Not even a good old Oregon rainstorm. Instead, the air was heavy with the acrid smoke of a nearby outdoor copra-drying oven.

There was almost nothing to remind us of Christmas . . . except the holiday letters from home, letters filled with sorrow and pity that we had to be so far away at Christmastime . . . except the pile of gaily-wrapped packages propped up beside our scrawny native Christmas tree . . . except for the raucous, untrained voices of children singing "Christmas carols" outside my gate—musical ministrations accompanied by the banging of empty tin cans and kettle covers. Ah yes, the annual charity drive! A "Merry Christmas," the outstretched hands, and the banging at the gate reminded us. If we did not come up with a "Christmas donation," there would be no peace on Earth tonight or any night until after the Feast of the Three Kings in early January.

I tucked my three children into their beds on Christmas Eve. They were excited and not at all inclined to settle down for a long winter's nap. When they had finally quieted down, I slipped out of their room and walked out into the fragrant, darkened garden. A restless wind rustled through the palm fronds.

So this was Christmas.

Sadness descended on me, a stab of loneliness. Self pity? There was no denying it. Here we were so far away from family, friends, and familiar traditions on Christmas Eve.

My wife's call from the front door reminded me that we must hurry to fulfill our commitment to a small, nearby church. We carried our folding pump organ between us. I walked in front, holding a kerosene lantern in my free hand. Silent in our own thoughts, we crossed the rice paddies toward the little lakeside fishing village of Victoria, making our way in the palm-framed moonlight from one terrace wall to another.

Seemed a little crazy to start a children's Christmas program just one hour before midnight! But we had promised. Sonia would play the pump organ, accompanying the congregation in their carols and the children in their special Christmas solos, duets, and choirs. My task was to bring Christmas greetings, done with little confidence in my halting Tagalog, and to share a brief Christmas meditation.

The church was already filled when we arrived, dimly lit with the few kerosene lanterns available. Broad-shouldered fishermen reached out water-roughened hands to corral errant children. Mothers, dressed in their simple "finery" applied one more stroke and pat of make-up, not upon themselves, but upon their children. Stooped and weathered grandmothers alternately bestowed approving smiles and corrective scowls upon the excited children.

The program began. Restless in their excitement, the crowd craned necks and shifted in chairs, awaiting their favorite thespian performance or childish aria. I looked out through the open window. The moon tucked itself behind a cloud, making the stars shine brighter. For just a moment I felt transported both in time and space to another starlit night. The music from the chapel platform now sounded like the anthems of heavenly choirs; midget shepherds wrapped brightly in mother's discarded robes took on the appearance of "shepherds in the field, keeping their watch by night." The precocious little girl in the too-large costume actually became the angel announcing "good tidings of great joy."

I watched in wonder as small children, the sons and daughters of simple, poor fishermen told with a growing rapture the miracle of that first Christmas day.

And I knew! I knew that rather than suffering the deprivation of a holiday in a strange land separated by great distances from family and friends, this Christmas would live in my heart for all time as the most joyous Christmas celebration of all.

Life is so often like that. We give, or "give up," only to discover that we receive so much more in return. Imagined voluntary deprivations become means for spontaneous, authentic celebrations that bring far greater heart-satisfaction than all our carefully contrived plans could ever deliver. This realization has provided me emotional equilibrium when I have been exposed to so much human suffering. Amazingly, it is among the world's poorest that I have often discovered life's greatest joys. Not at overflowing banquet tables, but in tiny rooms of native huts, at simple meals shared as a token of thanksgiving and heartfelt appreciation for friendship and caring.

Here is what the world is looking for! Genuine joy. Deep satisfaction. Spontaneous celebration. You can't buy it and you can't contrive it, but if you look in the right places, you may find yourself right in the midst of it.

Chances are good, however, that the rich will never find it. Encumbered by their possessions and investments, they are all too often the ones too busy, too anxious, too distracted, and too burdened to enter into the true celebration of life.

What they gain in gathering possessions and "security" is nothing in comparison to what they lose.

Free At Last! Free At Last!

On the night of his assassination, Martin Luther King had addressed a gathering of Memphis, Tennessee, garbage collectors. He had "been to the mountain," he told them. He felt free from the fear of death; he felt a total abandonment to the will of God. Rather than being imprisoned by concerns for personal safety, he seemed liberated by a celebration of hope.

"Free at last! Free at last! Thank God Almighty, I am free at last!"

Hours later his crumpled body gasped its final breaths on the second floor balcony of a seedy Memphis motel. Free of personal expectations and with a perspective of the eternal formed by both the defeats and victories of the civil rights movement, Dr. King had learned that:

"It is in giving we receive . . .
it is in dying we are born to eternal life."

In March of 1980, eighty-five Christians from twenty-seven countries gathered in Hoddesdon, England, to consider questions of personal freedom and personal resources. They had before them the 1974 Lausanne Covenant which called on believers around the world to "develop a simple life style."

What did that phrase mean? Was it biblical? What were its implications?

For four days they talked and listened—to each other and to the voice of God. Through the pages of the Bible they heard the cries of the hungering poor. Affirming that God's creation is marked by rich abundance and diversity, they acknowledged their responsibility of stewardship to husband these resources and share them freely. While acknowledging that "involuntary poverty is an offense against the goodness of God," they expressed belief that Jesus still calls some people to follow him in a life style of total, voluntary poverty. They discussed the implications of "community" within the worldwide Church. They were open with each other about their own personal struggles to reflect more Christlike life styles.

Concluding their four days of study, introspection, and interpretation, they expressed their shared resolve:

"So then, *having been freed* by the sacrifice of our Lord Jesus Christ . . . we humbly commit ourselves to develop a just and simple life style, to support one another in it and to encourage others to join us in this commitment."

They concluded their deliberations with a joyous celebration.

"Free at last! Free at last! Thank God Almighty, I am free at last!"

Yugoslav writer Mihajlo Jihajlov, who spent some years in a Yugoslavian jail, cites case after case of people like Solzhenitsyn and others who say that they first experienced true freedom in the confines of dreary prisons and cruel forced-labor camps. It was only after they lost their freedom that they finally understood what that freedom had meant. It was only after their futures were forcibly taken from them that they discovered a profound and compelling purpose for living. When given the choice of saving soul or body, those who chose to save their souls discovered that their bodies gained strength by that choice.

All of this fulfills precisely what our Lord said . . . he who hates his life in this world shall keep it for all eternity . . . and he who loves his life in this world will assuredly lose it.

CLINGING OR CELEBRATING?

Why is it, then, that we cling so ferociously to what we possess? What keeps us from celebrating the freedom which comes to those who surrender all but the essentials of life to God? John Wesley once remarked, "Christians should give away all but the 'plain necessaries of life,' that is, plain whole-some food, clean clothes and enough to carry on one's business and provide responsibly for the future. . . . Any Christian who takes for himself anything more than 'the plain necessaries of life' lives in an open, habitual denial of the Lord . . . he has gained riches and hell-fire!"

Spoken with integrity by one who purportedly earned 1400 pounds yearly on books he had published, spent a mere 30 pounds yearly for his own special interests, and gave the remainder to the poor! How many of us have discovered a certain "hell-fire" in the anxieties and cares which multiply as our net worth grows. Encumbered with many things, we lose our joy in relationships, our celebration in simply living. Clinging to that which we know to be worthless in the light of eternal values, we lose a bit of our very souls.

A simple life style need not become a new legalism. Lived out wisely, it has all the potential to impart a new sense of liberation.

Look back on the Lord's designated Year of Jubilee for the people of Israel. Now there was a celebration with real life style implications! Jubilee was that year during which land would revert to its former owners, because "the land is mine and you are but aliens and my tenants" (Leviticus 25:23). Gaining a proper perspective on ownership of resources frees us from our enslavement to what we possess and liberates us to live in love and faith, in hope and caring. The slaves set free in our year of Jubilee may very well be ourselves!

Jehovah told Israel, "If one of your countrymen becomes poor and is unable to support himself among you, help him as you would an alien or a temporary resident." Contrary to our modern myths, this quality of generous, voluntary sharing does not breed dependence but rather encourages a healthy spirit of *interdependence*. It was "out of their *overflowing joy* and *extreme poverty*" that the Macedonian believers voluntarily shared with their famine-stricken brothers and sisters in Jerusalem. They pleaded with the apostle Paul "for the privilege of sharing in this service to the saints" (2 Corinthians 8:2-4). Jubilee! And here the Lord's messenger established an important principle:

> Our desire is not that others might be relieved while you are hard pressed, but that there might be equality. At the present time your plenty will supply what they need, so that in turn their plenty will supply what you need. Then there will be equality, as it is written: "He that gathered much did not have too much, and he that gathered little did not have too little" (2 Corinthians 8:13-15).

Jubilee! Let us celebrate our opportunities to share rather than dreading those feelings of obligation and guilt we all feel when we experience another's poverty in our abundance.

Blaise Pascal writes: "The great and the humble have the same misfortunes, the same griefs, the same passions, but the one is at the top of the wheel, and the other near the center, and so less disturbed by the same revolutions."

Reaching out from our "center," we can do so much to keep those on the outer rim from being crushed by the pressures and deprivations of life. It comes down to this:

Living with less . . . so that others might live. This is Jubilee!

BALANCING LIFE'S PRIORITIES

Reared in a poor third-world country by missionary parents, Matt returned to the United States for his education. Just when his plans for study and career seemed close to fulfillment,

Matt received tragic news from his parents' adopted country: His father had been killed in a car accident.

Shaken, Matt carefully evaluated his own career plans. Did his theological education really represent God's best plan for his future? The more he thought and prayed about it, the more he felt drawn—actually *compelled*—to move in a different direction. It wasn't long before Matt was making major strides in the commercial world. With a sense of divine call in his ability to earn and manage money, Matt's skills in the commodity market brought him wealth.

Matt met me at the airport one evening in his beat-up 1977 Buick. I felt a little shame when I remembered my much newer Honda. We sat around the kitchen table that night in his modest suburban home as he queried me about the most urgent needs from "my world." Before the evening was finished, Matt had committed a large sum of money to serve specific needs of the poor and to serve them in Jesus' name.

Matt lives simply and finds life immensely enjoyable. His eyes danced with excitement as he familiarized himself with the various projects I presented that night. He planned his financial involvement with a joy that bordered on hilarity.

When vacation time comes, Matt plans excursions to some of the most impoverished areas in the whole world. His hobbies? Planning and marketing technological innovations which will help transport missionaries in remote areas . . . or help farmers with few resources use simple technical advances that will make it possible for them to grow their own food. He freely shares his business acumen with third-world Christian entrepreneurs, helping them develop markets for their cottage-industry produced products.

What a joyful time Matt and I experienced that night in his home! I was in the presence of a man who had learned to balance priorities . . . a man who found life sweet, eminently worth living.

The Bible brims with real-life illustrations of men and women who learned to balance life's priorities. Abraham weighed the security of Ur against his "transfer" to an unknown and far away place called Canaan. Don't minimize the agony of that decision. Yet the patriarch had heard God's voice. He packed his bags for Canaan.

Moses turned his back on a stellar career and a life of ease in Pharoah's palace. For what? For the deprivations of a despised and captive people—who just happened to be God's people. There is no record that he ever looked back.

Nehemiah left the unbelievable luxuries of Babylon and a position in the emperor's "inner circle" to journey to a charred and broken city on the backside of the empire—a city that just happened to be God's city. He rolled up his expensive sleeves and went to work as a wall builder, serving a King greater than the one he had left behind.

Easy choices? Not by any measure! Yet these men had learned to balance the priorities of life—and their names are inscribed forever in God's Book.

Learning how to give up one's rights or possessions when those resources are best spent for others *is* learning to balance life's priorities. It's never easy. But everywhere I have encountered this open-handed, open-hearted attitude, I have seen authentic celebration . . . and unshakable joy.

MOVING TOWARD COMMITMENT

Luther Gerlach and Virginia Hine, in their book *People, Power, Change,* observe that there are certain predictable and shared manifestations of commitment:

They note that "strongly held convictions generate an almost impervious sense of assurance." It is not surprising, then, that strength of conviction is often considered synonymous with commitment. When we really believe, like Gandhi, that "this world has enough for every man's need, but not enough for every man's greed," our convictions will move us toward a commitment which declares, "the end of hunger is an idea whose time has come."

In those entering the commitment process, there is always "a capacity for risk-taking." This goes beyond giving out of the security of one's assured resources. It means risking what you now possess in order to respond to the need of those with no possessions. After more than thirty-two years in Christian service, my wife and I have *never* arrived at a point where there is no risk-taking in our giving. But it is living here on the edge of adventure that we find life's greatest satisfaction. The gift which costs us nothing returns to us little (if any) reward.

When people become participants through personal commitment to important causes, inevitable behavioral changes result. Commitments which do not result in behavioral changes are only expressions of desire—not of will. True commitment must be measured in terms of action. There is no other measure. God so loved the world that he did something about it—he sent his only begotten Son. Eternity itself hinges on the commitment Jesus Christ made to you and me. He didn't just speak words, he became the Word.

> [He] made himself nothing,
>> taking the very nature of a servant,
>> being made in human likeness. . . .
>> he humbled himself . . .
>> became obedient to death—
>>> even death on a cross!
>>> (Philippians 2:7,8).

Personal commitments are something more than fine words and worthy sentiments. There is a price to be paid. And if we would become instruments of healing and reconciliation, share freely of personal resources, and stand bravely for justice, we must be prepared to stand the cost.

COME TO THE PARTY!

Jesus invites us to an incredible celebration:

A celebration of those who give up everything to gain everything.

A celebration where you die in order to live.

A celebration where your abundance is measured not by what you control, but by what he promises to those who have yielded control.

"He who gives to the poor," writes the wise man, "will lack nothing, but he who closes his eyes to them receives many curses" (Proverbs 28:27).

Who has the stooped shoulders and the dark rings around the eyes? Is it the poor family one finds in a remote village of India, where together in their poverty they share *all that they have* in order to celebrate together some marriage, birthday, or special national holiday? Or is it the harried businessman, the hurried executive, the hapless investor who has placed all his confidence in profits, career goals, and balance sheets—yet finds himself "troubled with the cares of this life"? Sure, this wealthy one knows where his next meal is coming from, but he will eat it with no sense of celebration! His very joy, security, and sense of well-being are tied to such fickle trivialities as declining stock markets, rising investment costs, turn-downs in the economy, and sluggishness in the market-place.

> When we understand our world, with its
> > pain,
> > sorrow,
> > injustice,
> > and dying . . .
>
> when we understand God's perfect plan for his creation:
> > life and health,
> > salvation,
> > justice, and
> > joy . . .
>
> when we discover that life's abundance is not experienced in the accumulation of things:
> > cars and houses,

appliances and appurtenances,
swimming pools and sport palaces . . .

but rather in
relationships
and
essentials for living
and
attitudes which contribute to celebration . . .

then we have found that place of *true* well-being.

We are on the way to experiencing life as God has promised it, life lived in abundance.

When resources flow like a stream from our hands to other hands, from our heart to other hearts, life stays sweet and refreshing—clean and pure. With God as its source, it is a stream that will never run dry!

Scripture Index

Subject Index